In Place of the Flawed Diamond

American University Studies

Series V
Philosophy

Vol. 13

PETER LANG

New York · Berne · Frankfurt am Main

Peter J. Hadreas

In Place of the
Flawed Diamond

An Investigation of Merleau-Ponty's Philosophy

PETER LANG
New York · Berne · Frankfurt am Main

Library of Congress Cataloging in Publication Data

Hadreas, Peter J.:
In Place of the Flawed Diamond.

(American University Studies.   Series V, Philosophy; vol. 13)
Bibliography: p.
1. Merleau-Ponty, Maurice, 1908–1961.   I. Title.
II. Series: American University Studies. Series V, Philosophy; v. 13.
B2430.M3764H33   1986   194   86-7241
ISBN 0-8204-0211-7
ISSN 0739-6392

CIP-Kurztitelaufnahme der Deutschen Bibliothek

Hadreas, Peter J.:
In Place of the Flawed Diamond: An Investigation
of Merleau-Ponty's Philosophy / Peter J. Hadreas. –
New York; Berne; Frankfurt am Main: Lang,
1986.
(American University Studies: Ser. 5,
Philosophy; Vol. 13)
ISBN 0-8204-0211-7

NE: American University Studies / 05

© Peter Lang Publishing, Inc., New York 1986

Printed by Lang Druck, Inc., Liebefeld/Berne (Switzerland)

To my Mother, Father and Susan,
in gratitude

Contents

Page

Abbreviations xiii

INTRODUCTION:
1. The problem of a philosophical commentary which
   is presented as a personal intellectual narrative. 1

CHAPTER ONE: *The Structure of Behavior* and the
   liberation of Gestalt from the ontology of Gestalt
   psychology 13

1. The stimulus-response model as an attempt to
   introduce causality and thus "science" into theories
   of behavior 16
2. The three structures of behavior 19
   The syncretic form 19
   The amovable form 20
   The symbolic form 22
3. The physical, vital, and human orders and the first
   answer to the mind/body problem 24
4. Gestalt and intentionality are implicitly
   reconceived 33

CHAPTER TWO: *The Phenomenology of Perception*:
   The body-subject and its pact with the natural
   world 41

1. *In Place of the Flawed Diamond* 41
2. The "thingliness" of the thing: Heidegger's account
   and its similarity to Merleau-Ponty's 43

3. The distinction between the objective and the pre-objective worlds 49
4. The criticism of the Empiricist and Rationalist approaches to Perception 52
5. A difficulty in establishing the intellectual influences of Merleau-Ponty's theory of the body-subject. 60
6. What the body-subject is not 63
7. The "pact" formed between the body-subject and the natural world 64
8. The anonymity of the body-subject: the pre-personal one 78
9. The directionality of the body-subject and the unity of the natural world 80
10. Does Merleau-Ponty have a theory of authenticity in *The Phenomenology of Perception?* 89

CHAPTER THREE: The foundations of language and reflection 95

1. Merleau-Ponty's revision of Husserl's *Fundierung* relation 95
2. The interpenetration of language and the body 99
3. The foundation of language in the body: neither sublimation nor reduction 105
4. Radical reflection is not adduced by a disinvolved subject 112
5. Eternity, "the atmosphere of time:" eternity and temporality are reciprocally founded 116
6. Radical reflection as self-reflecting authentic expression which is aware of its origins 120

CHAPTER FOUR: *The Visible and The Invisible* and the Discovery of the Chiasm 129

1. The fundamental pattern which adumbrates Being: the chiasm. 133
2. The chiasm as an ontological element: the flesh 141

3. The unavailability of Merleau-Ponty's later thought
   to representational thinking 149
4. Further regions of the flesh and the chiasm: a new
   approach to the philosophy of history and mind 154

BIBLIOGRAPHY 162

Acknowledgment

I would like to acknowledge Professor John Chioles for encouraging me to work on this book and for following its progress with much helpful advice. I wish to extend thanks to Susan Telcher who read over the drafts and helped with the editing. Last, I would also like to thank Dr. Joanne de Philips who offered her singular helpfulness and support during the writing of this book.

Abbreviations

References to Merleau-Ponty's work appear in parenthesis in the text. References to the French text alone indicate that the translation is my own.

CAL   *Consciousness and the Acquisition of Language,* translated by Hugh J. Silvermann, Northwestern University Press, 1973, Evanston

EM   "The Eye and the Mind" in *The Primacy of Perception,* Northwestern University Press, 1964, Evanston

Ph.P   *The Phenomenology of Perception,* translated by Colin Smith, revised by Forrest Williams, Routledge and Kegan Paul, 1962, London

PP   *Phénoménologie de la perception,* Gallimard, 1945, Paris

S   *Signes,* Gallimard, 1960, Paris

SB   *The Structure of Behavior,* translated by A. L. Fisher, forward by J. Wild, Beacon Press, 1963, Boston

SC   *La structure de comportement,* Second Edition forward by A. De Waehlens, Universitaires de France, 1967, Paris

Signs   *Signs,* translation and introduction by McClearly, Northwestern University Press, 1968, Evanston

SNS   *Sense and Non-Sense*, translation and introduction by H. L. Dreyfus and P. A. Dreyfus, Northwestern University Press, 1964, Evanston

SNS   *Sens et non-sens*, Nagel, 1966, Paris

VI   *The Visible and the Invisible*, edited by Clade Lefort, translated by Alphonso Lingis, Northwestern University Press, 1968, Evanston

VI   *Le visible et l'invisible: suivi de notes de travail*, text established by Claude Lefort, Gallimard, 1964, Paris

Introduction

1. The problem of a philosophical commentary which is presented as a personal intellectual narrative.

In Gary Madison's study of Merleau-Ponty's work, *The Phenomenology of Merleau-Ponty*,[1] Madison points out that although only a few years separate the completion of *The Structure of Behavior* and *The Phenomenology of Perception* "readers cannot but note the great difference in tone between the two essays."[2] *The Structure of Behavior* "begins with a critical study of experimental psychology, behaviorism, and Gestalt psychology, and then develops into a critical reflection on these sciences." *The Phenomenology of Perception*, on the other hand, true to its title, answers the questions which the *Structure of Behavior* raises by continuing the inquiry on the level of "natural and unsophisticated experience."[3] Madison goes on later to emphasize that the difference between *The Phenomenology of Perception* and Merleau-Ponty's last work, *The Visible and the Invisible* is even more fundamental. Merleau-Ponty in these two books passes from "positive phenomenology" (Ph.P, p. xvii; PP p. xii) to "negative ontology" (See VI, p. 179 or Madison, p. 195). The force of the later passage into ontology is described dramatically: Madison speaks of a "radical calling into question", the setting up of "a wholly new starting point," "a total taking up again of the *Phenomenology of Perception*."[4]

That Merleau-Ponty's main works shift profoundly in methodological orientation and conception of philosophy itself, is hardly a matter of dispute. I would like to point out however that

1

Madison's presentation, which I might add in my opinion is a valuable piece of scholarship, takes a "personal intellectual narrative" as its format. This, I should note, is not Madison's claim. He intends his study to be "an interpretive reappropriation." But there is a bit of romance in this description. We know of the expression "interpretive reappropriation," if we make sense of it at all, by importing elements of Heidegger's way of talking about philosophy. Heidegger's study of Kant is a case of "interpretive reappropriation." Heidegger shows, through his interpretation of Kant, how Kant's particular manner of reappropriating being is a way of "owning" Kant's philosophy freshly and illuminates anew Kant's position in the history of Western thought. Madison, on the other hand, in making his contribution to Merleau-Ponty scholarship is doing something much more conventional. He is giving us a "story," an intellectual narrative. I do not mean to single out Madison here for his approach. It is taken for granted as a way of organizing a philosopher's work. One can find similar approaches throughout the critical literature which treats major thinkers. Typical examples would be Pears', *Ludwig Wittgenstein* and Kaufmann's, *Hegel*.[6]

The personal intellectual narrative approach preselects what will count as relevant. Let me explain. The intellectual narrative, of which I am using Madison's book as a good example, suggests that a thinker's development may be understood as a conversation the thinker has over his career with himself or with other thinkers. Thus in an often quoted working note, Merleau-Ponty writes to himself in his preparation for writing *The Visible and the Invisible*, "The problems posed in *Ph.P* are insoluble because I start from the 'consciousness'-'object' distinction" (VI, 200; *VI*, 237). From this note, we see that Merleau-Ponty has rethought his earlier work and is about to reform it; thus this note marks an important point in the account of the philosopher's intellectual narrative. But of course a philosopher's development is not dependent only upon his own self-criticism. The second main part of the intellectual narrative is the influence of other thinkers. Accordingly, Madison points out the powerful effect of Heidegger's later thought on Merleau-Ponty's final work. As he states: "It is a fact—upon which almost all commentators are agreed—that Merleau-Ponty became more and more interested in Heideggerian thought, in the thought of the later Heidegger."[7] So in accordance with this plan, Madison's book, like many works that discuss the views of a thinker, does so by presenting the thinker as ruminating over the fruits of his own thought, while at the same time surrendering, usually in two or three key turning points, to the researches of another thinker, who becomes through some manner of emulation, simulation, or contest, an additional character in the dialogue which expresses the thinker's views.

What if anything is wrong with this approach? As I indicated this approach preselects what material will count as relevant. It does so in various ways. First the intellectual narrative prescribes a view of the thinker's development which casts his work as a dialogue between himself and other seminal thinkers. In the case of philosophy, and I think also mathematics, there are special reasons for endorsing this view. The philosopher, after all, is dealing with topics that few people can or care to discuss in a way that has much to do with the topic. Moreover, major philosophers are usually at the front ranks of developing new approaches to philosophical problems. But it takes time to absorb new ideas. Few professional philosophers have the opportunity to respond without considerable time lag to truly innovative ideas. So the philosopher's development does tend to involve, in fact, a limited number of participants.

But the intellectualist narrative approach does not only suggest that a small number of influences are relevant; it also tends to presume an autonomy of thought among various thinkers. The plan sets up a lineage of influences. The thinkers which play into the development of a philosopher's development are treated like members of a family tree who are wholly responsible for the genes of their remarkable heir. By this I do not only mean to suggest that within the personal intellectual narrative, sociological, political and historical influences tend to be thought of as belonging to another domain of criticism. But that thought

3

itself—even sociological, political or historical thought—is presumed to proceed from the mind of certain philosophic geniuses whose genius is awakened by other philosophic geniuses. Now the extreme individualism inherent in this schema is contemporaneously being questioned by various works of criticism deriving from second generation ordinary language philosophers or from various philosophers taking a hermeneutical approach. Here, the *dramatis personae* of the thinker's development are not essentially individuals but rather those who count as spokesmen for important shifts in language or cultural practices. So Richard Rorty's influential book, *Philosophy and the Mirror of Nature*[8] is less an account of how main thinkers of the Anglo-American tradition made developments upon each other's thought, as it is a chronicle of ways in which important philosophers continued to become enmeshed in certain traps instituted by centuries of misguided philosophic discourse. Foucault's later work, at least in approach, is similar. In works such as *A History of Sexuality*,[9] the notion of sexuality is shown to have a geneology. It is born out of cultural roots in the 19th Century which in Foucault's view admit of division neither by individual nor classes. It is not a question of Freud's inventing a theory of sexuality which Ferenczi develops and which Adler reconceives. The notion of sexuality is cast from a working of new significations upon older significations, as a culture finds new circuits by which it might increase its directedness and scope of power. For Foucault, it is reasonable to say that Freud did not discover that sexuality and character are correlatable. No, rather, this correlation discovered him.

Thus one criticism that can be made of the intellectual narrative is its tendency to account for the development of a thinker according to the interworking of various autonomous philosophic geniuses or at least very bright minds. But a second criticism arises as one considers special cases among philosophers. Philosophers often include their own account of the development of their ideas, and this account can be elemental in the interpretation of their views. Because of the naïveté involved, we are inclined to forget that Aristotle and Hegel, for

4

example, both saw themselves as the fulfillment of a tradition which had prepared the way for their thought. In *The Metaphysics*, Aristotle indicates that previous philosophers had the four causes only vaguely or in part; thus, they could only give partial accounts. But since Aristotle claims that he alone perceived clearly the four causes, his inquiries alone are complete.[10] And Hegel indicates that his charting of the realization of "The Absolute" in *The Phenomenology of Spirit* was contemporaneous with his noting it. Thus, in his view, he becomes the spokesman for the culmination of history and thought.[11]

Merleau-Ponty, I believe, presents a special problem in regard to his own account of his development particularly because of this second feature of the intellectual narrative. Almost antipodal to the assessment of an Aristotle or a Hegel, Merleau-Ponty does not incorporate into his analysis a reflection which ascribes to himself a position in the history of his fields. On the contrary, he makes other thinkers into the representatives of his ideas. I believe, this account—his own intellectual narrative—hides what is particularly innovative in Merleau-Ponty's thought behind the thought of his intellectual influences. And this, I will argue, leads me to pose a particular approach for discussing his work.

How is Merleau-Ponty's account of the development of his own views withheld? Let us take an example. In *The Phenenology of Perception*, Merleau-Ponty makes much use of a notion of intentionality which he finds in Husserl's later writings i.e. operative or *fungierende* intentionality. Merleau-Ponty repeatedly indicates that this view of intentionality brings Husserl to the notion of human existence as "involvement" in the Heideggerian sense. That Merleau-Ponty found an existential significance in Husserl's later writings is very odd indeed. It is sometimes explained by pointing out that Merleau-Ponty approached Husserl through the work of one of Husserl's students, Eugene Fink, who emphasized Husserl's move from "intentionality of act" to operative intentionality. Thus Merleau-Ponty states in *The Phenomenology of Perception,* footnoting Fink's critical article:

In Husserl's language, beneath the 'intentionality of the act', which is the thetic consciousness of the object, and which, in intellectual memory for example, converts 'this' into an idea, we must recognize an 'operative' intentionality (*fungierende Intentionalität*) which makes the former possible, and which is what Heidegger terms transcendence. (Ph.P, 418; PP, 478)

But the fact is that Husserl's explicit views as well as Fink's interpretation of Husserl's views are fundamentally alien to Heidegger's approach. Husserl's operative intentionality is not Heidegger's notion of transcendence. Far from it. Heidegger says explicitly in *Being and Time* in a section subtitled "The Temporal Problem of the Transcendence of the World":

The 'problem of transcendence' cannot be brought round to the question of how a subject comes out to an Object, where the aggregate of objects is identified with the idea of the world.[12]

"Transcendence," as Heidegger refers to it, is directed to a horizon and to the "clearing." This not what Husserl had in mind since Husserl's operative intentionality still implies a transcendental subject which *constitutes* a world.[13] So then for the sake of telling our intellectual narrative, we are led to ask the question: "Why did Merleau-Ponty claim that Husserl's view came to express a position similar to Heidegger's. Did Merleau-Ponty simply misread Husserl or Fink? How did the formative dialogue between these thinkers take place? We should also reflect, in asking this question, how are we presuming an answer along the lines of an intellectual narrative?

In the preface to the *The Phenomenology of Perception*, Merleau-Ponty discusses, point by point, main issues of phenomenology. He discusses: 1) phenomenology's claim to be a descriptive psychology, 2) the phenomenological reduction, 3) the eidetic reduction, and 4) intentionality. He discusses these seminal issues with the intention of indicating the "true meaning" (Ph.P, p. xi; PP p. v) of these doctrines. Along these lines, he points out that "descriptive psychology" of the phenomenological sort reveals that "The world is not an object such that I have in my possession the law of its making; it is the natural setting of, and field for, all my thoughts and all my explicit perceptions." (Ph.P, p. xi; PP p. v) He indicates that the phenomenological reduction reveals that one is inextricably "in the world" in the Heideggerian sense. He points out that the eidetic reduction, apart from separating essences from existence, shows how "the possible is based on the real." (Ph.P, p. xvii; PP p. xii). And he holds that Husserl's distinction between intentionality of act and operative intentionality illuminates the fact that our relationship to the world "is not a thing which can be any further clarified by analysis; philosophy can only place it once more before our eyes and present it for our ratification." (Ph.P, p. xviii; PP p. xiii) Merleau-Ponty in this discussion does not indicate a misreading of Husserl—he deals point by point with conventional interpretations of Husserl. The fact is that although he is aware of the conventional readings of Husserl; he chooses to reject them. Rather he finds in Husserl what Husserl's research, and in particular Husserl's failures, have revealed *to him*, not Husserl. But, he then reads these disclosures, in each case brilliant but having little to do with Husserl himself, back into Husserl. In short, he makes his predecessor into the spokeman for his own ideas.

There is a similar situation in *The Structure of Behavior*. In *The Structure of Behavior*, Merleau-Ponty attributes to the psychologists of "form," the Gestaltists, Weisacker, Goldstein, Wertheimer, Kohler and Koffka, the seminal notion which will allow for an account of behavior which avoids the classical antinomies of soul and body. As he states:

> . . . We would like to return to the notion of form, to seek out in what sense forms can be said to exist "in" the physical world and "in" the living body, and to ask of form itself the solution to the antinomy of which it is the occasion, the synthesis of matter and idea. (SB, p. 137; SC, p. 147)

But the solution he offers, which we will discuss in greater detail later, involves an instance of form which one cannot find

7

in any of the Gestaltists he draws upon. Merleau-Ponty's use of form, as discussed in his accounting for particularly human behavior for example, already involves his concept of *vertical significance* wherein new meaning is built upon old in a way that both overcomes and preserves the earlier expression. (See SB, p. 176; SC, p. 190). The concept of form which he imports from the Gestaltists is too simplistic to account for his notion of "the human order." The long and short of it is that Merleau-Ponty is again reading back into major intellectual influences his own remarkable innovations. It is as if Merleau-Ponty is repeatedly writing his work "for hire," attributing ownership to intellectual forbears who have employed him to write in their name.

In his last work, *The Visible and the Invisible*, he is more openly and honestly critical of his sources of influence. He criticizes at length Sartre's ontology which could idealize the concepts of being and nothingness and directly opposes various of Husserl's doctrines. But I cannot find anything but a distortion of the truth in the claim of G. Granel, who describes Merleau-Ponty's relation to Husserl as ". . . the ritual killing of the Father, which Merleau-Ponty was in the process of committing, piously and pitilessly, and which would be something over and done with if he had not himself died."[14] *The Visible and the Invisible* is appended with 103 "Working Notes," often pages long, wherein Merleau-Ponty records thoughts which he was occupied with in developing the manuscript of his final work. Over thirty of these notes discuss Husserlian notions. His attitude towards Husserl, for the most part, is revisionary. But he still draws upon Husserl as a source from which he may establish his own views, which are, as often as not, Husserl transformed, and not, as Granel's characterization would imply, Husserl disposed of. In short, I wish to argue that even in Merleau-Ponty's last work, wherein he does tend to present more than ever before his own innovations as just that, his tendency is still to present his insights as if they were interpretations—the *Ungedacht*—of the writings of others.

Now by remarking upon this peculiarity of Merleau-Ponty writings—the curious way in which he casts his own thought into the work of his predecessors—I do not mean to minimize the role of such major influences as Husserl or Heidegger on his work. What I am claiming is rather that the intellectual narrative that Merleau-Ponty endorses and which many commentators follow is deceptive. First it tends to de-emphasize some of his most brilliant contributions by identifying them with views of Husserl, Heidegger or the Gestaltists. Second it obscures the fact that the sources of these ideas were likely much more broad and quixotic than the intellectual narrative with its narrowly confined lineage of influences permits us to admit.

Thus, we are brought to consider a way of treating Merleau-Ponty's work which will take into account this peculiarity of his presenting his own views. In this book I will be dealing primarily with the three main publications of his work, *The Structure of Behavior*, *The Phenomenology of Perception*, and *The Visible and the Invisible*. (The last work was left unfinished. But it was found containing, along with several hundred pages of working notes, a written out manuscript of over a hundred pages.) I will be avoiding the personal intellectual narrative approach. Rather, I will try to expose what is particularly original in these three books, hoping that the reader will bear in mind that such a dissection, although likely to set Merleau-Ponty's genius on display, will do some injustice to his own manner of presentation. In particular, in regards to *The Structure of Behavior* I will be interested primarily in discussions of the "human order" and how Merleau-Ponty uses it to account for mind-body relations. In the *Phenomenology of Perception* I will be occupied primarily in his view of the body-subject. I would like to draw out aspects of his view that are often missed by commentators, namely, ways in which his theory of the body leads him to arrive at an original version of "being-in-the-world" as formed by the "pact" between the body-subject and the natural world. I will take up another chapter discussing his rediscovery of the foundations of language and reflection in his development of Husserl's *Fundierung* relation. (Here again he attributes to Husserl his own innovations and revisions.) Last, in *The Visible and the Invisible* I will be primarily concerned with his last most remarkable contribution, the notion of the "chiasma" and how this highly original notion allowed him to deal freshly with not only the subject/object ontology but with ontology in general. Recurrently in the book I will be introducing Heidegger's views on specific topics. Less often I will introduce Sartre's or Husserl's. My intention here will not be to indicate influences as much as point out how Merleau-Ponty's views differ from these major figures of his tradition.

It was Merleau-Ponty's plan in all three books, to present first the prejudices of a tradition and indicate how these prejudices misguided the investigation of fundamental phenomena. Thus in *The Structure of Behavior*, he prepares his account of the structure of behavior arguing against the mechanism presumed in stimulus-response accounts of behavior and in the physiology of "the central sector." In *The Phenomenology of Perception* his lengthy introduction sets about to expose the *prèjugé du monde*, i.e. the tendency to explain the world through the collection of atomic bits of data or by mentalistic processes which organize atomic bits of data. In the *Visible and the Invisible*, he takes up the prejudices implied by three mistaken accounts of interrogation, all of which misconceive the nature of interrogation and thus of philosophical questioning itself. Each of these accounts of methodological and ontological prejudices is worthy of a book in itself. In this book however, since I will be concerned with those thoughts which are formative of his own positive views, I will only be dealing with these sections insofar as they relate to the exposition of his view on the "human order," "the body-subject" or the "chiasma."

Notes to the Introduction

[1] Madison, Gray Brent, *The Phenomenology of Merleau-Ponty*. Ohio University Press, Athens, Ohio, 1981.

[2] op. cit. p. 2

[3] op. cit. p. 18. (Madison is quoting de Waelhens)

[4] op. cit. pp. 167–8

[5] op. cit. p. xxxii

10

[6] Bibliographical information on the two books mentioned is as follows: Pears, David, *Ludwig Wittgenstein*, New York, The Viking Press, 1969; Kaufmann, Walter, *Hegel, Reinterpretation, Text and Commentary*, Doubleday, 1965, New York

[7] Madison, op. cit. p. 252

[8] Rorty, Richard, *Philosophy and the Mirror of Nature*, Princeton University Press, 1979, Princeton.

[9] Foucault, Michel, *A History of Sexuality Vol. I: An Introduction*, 1980, Random House, New York

[10] *Metaphysics*, A, Chapter 10, 993all–15.

[11] See in particular sections 798 to 803 in *The Phenomenology of Spirit*, in, for example, the Miller translation, Clarendon Press, Oxford, 1977.

[12] Heidegger, M., *Being and Time*, Harper and Row, 1962, New York, p. 417

[13] Fink himself says in an article quoted by Merleau-Ponty: "The true theme of phenomenology is neither the world on the one hand, nor a transcendental subjectivity which is to be set over and against the world on the other, but the *world's becoming in the constitution of transcendental subjectivity*. (Fink's emphasis) From a translation of Fink's 1933 article, "Die phänomenologische Philosophie Edmund Husserls in der gegenwärtigen Kritik," which first appeared in *Kant-Studien* 38, pp. 319–383. A translation of this article has been made by R. O. Elveton and appears in his collection, *The Phenomenology of Husserl*, Quadrangle Books, 1970, Chicago.

[14] Granel, G., *Le sens du temps et de la perception chez E. Husserl*, Gallimard, Paris, 1968, p. 103.

1

The Structure of Behavior and the Liberation of Gestalt from the Ontology of Gestalt Psychology

Ultimately, El Greco's supposed visual disorder was conquered by him and so profoundly integrated in his manner of thinking and being that it appears finally as the necessary expression of his being much more than as a peculiarity imposed from the outside. It is no longer a paradox to say that "El Greco was astigmatic because he produced elongated bodies." Everything which was accidental in the individual, that is, everything which revealed partial and independent dialectics without relationship to the total signification of his life, has become assimilated and centered in his deeper life. Bodily events have ceased to constitute autonomous cycles, to follow the abstract patterns of biology and psychology, and have received a new meaning. It is nevertheless the body, it will be said, which in the final analysis explains El Greco's vision; his liberty consisted only in justifying this accident of nature by infusing it with a metaphysical meaning. (SB, p. 203; SC, p. 219)

I quote this description of El Greco's integration of his astigmatism into his world at length because El Greco's solution to his ocular abnormality counts as a remarkable accomplishment of what Merleau-Ponty calls "the human order." Merleau-Ponty's approach to the "human order" and human behavior in general is expressed in terms of refinements be brings to the notion of "Gestalt." It is fundamentally meta-psychological issues of Gestalt psychology that count as the main area Merleau-Ponty's innovations in *The Structure of Behavior*. And, it will be primarily these innovations which we will be concerned with in this chapter. Let us begin with distinguishing three different usages of Gestalt. The following three passages from

The Structure of Behavior reflect these differences. ("Form" is used interchangeably with "Gestalt" in *The Structure of Behavior*.)

> 1. The whole is not the sum of its parts. (SB, p. 150; SC, p. 163)
>
> 2. The form is a visible or sonorous configuration (or even a configuration prior to the distinction of the senses) in which the sensory value of each element is determined by its function in the whole and varies with it. (SB, p. 168; p. SC, 182).
>
> 3. By a natural development, the notion of 'Gestalt' led us back to its Hegelian meaning, that is to the concept before it has become consciousness of self. Nature, we said, is the exterior of a concept. But precisely the concept as concept has no exterior and the Gestalt still had to be conceptualized as a unity of the interior and exterior, of nature and idea. (SB, p. 210; SC, p. 227)

The first way of describing Gestalt is a formulaic one popular since the early researches of Ehrenfels into the primacy of perceptual wholes over their parts. Although it may have been useful as an encapsulation of the notion of Gestalt, it does not tell us very much about what a Gestalt is, and only very little about what it is not. Merleau-Ponty generally uses it as a rough way of signalling the notion of Gestalt for further elucidation. In fact, as a definition, its limitations are attested to by Merleau-Ponty in his later works. As he states for example in *The Visible and the Invisible* (VI, p. 204; *VI*, 258), it is merely "a negative, external definition".

The second passage cited above is one drawn from many where Merleau-Ponty endeavors to give a positive definition of Gestalt. As in the quote above (See also SB, p. 47; SC, 50 or SB, p. 91; SC, 101), this second account of Gestalt stresses the fact that no part, segment or element within a Gestalt has meaning or value *partes extra partes*. That is to say, each part has its value or significance only by relationship to other parts. Thus any change in the relationship between parts changes the Gestalt. On the other hand, if the relationships between the parts remain the same, for example all notes of a melody are raised a tone, the

14

form stays the same. In this second way of talking about Gestalt, a Gestalt expresses the constellation of relationships between parts. This usage accords with the standard usage of the notion of Gestalt among the Gestalt psychologists that Merleau-Ponty is engaged in examining.

The third way of defining Gestalt leads us to examine Merleau-Ponty's unique way of speaking of Gestalt. It is in line with this third notion of Gestalt that he employs the term "structure." As he states: "What is profound in the notion of 'Gestalt' from which we started is not the idea of signification but that of *structure*, the indiscernible joining of an idea and an existence, the contingent arrangement by which the materials coming before us have a sense, intelligibility in the nascent state" (SB, p. 206; SC, p. 223). The profundity that Merleau-Ponty refers to here arises from his own realization that apparent dichotomies of mind/body dualities may be reconsidered by noting that mentally, even in introspection, we are directed towards a world. Correlatively, the world which may seem to intrude upon us is discerned, selected, avoided, or sought after by us. When Merleau-Ponty, in the quote above refers to "the concept before it has become consciousness of self," he is using the Hegelian reference to lead us to conceive a mentalistic notion which nonetheless emerges from a non-mentalistic source, with which the mentalistic notion is in a dialectical relation. In short, he is alluding to Hegel's notion of a concept to lead us to a Gestalt as descriptive of consciousness/world dialectics in general.

Merleau-Ponty is prepared to conceive of mind/world dualities, like motor/perceptual relations, as interiors and exteriors of a Gestalt. The Gestalt in question is a form of behavior, which is conceived of as an equilibrium whose significance is subject to internal and external forces. Thus the notion of a "structure of behavior" presupposes that figure/ground perception is an exterior moment of an equilibrium which expresses the behavior of the organism as its interior moments lead it to "catch" or "comprehend" its world. The third sense of Gestalt which Merleau-Ponty employs here extends well beyond perception. In the third sense of Gestalt, organisms and their world *are* structures. Furthermore, organisms, Merleau-Ponty argues, can be classified according to three categorially different structures. It is in view of this third understanding of Gestalt that Merleau-Ponty's project in *The Structure of Behavior* can be assessed, that is, first, a specification of the three categorially different structures, and second, an accounting of how traditional problems of conceiving the integration of human nature—relations of mind to body—may be reconceived through the description of these structures.

1. The stimulus-response model as an attempt to introduce causality and thus "science" into theories of behavior—

A favorite model for those who wish to propose a "scientific" account for behavior is the model of a causal chain. How can the notion of a causal chain (a series of events whereby, for example, pressing a lever sets off a spring which vibrates a wire which rattles a plate, etc.) find any application in human behavior? In Merleau-Ponty's view stimulus-response theorists took advantage of this model. In particular, the reflex would seem to have the advantage of allowing for "the dignity of a cause." The impoverishment of the concept of the causal model in contemporary quantum or relativistic physics did not, as far as stimulus-response theories went, undo its claim to what is scientific—or perhaps one should say more properly "scientistic." In developing the theory of the reflex, a physiologist such as Sherrington proposed the classical version of a causal chain in behavior: A stimulus activates a receptor at a place of excitation, a reflex arc, i. e. a channeling in and out of a nerve center follows, and finally a resultant reaction at the end of the chain is brought about. This discovery had all the earmarks of physical mechanics. It seemed to provide the physiologist with a way to study one specific reaction of a human or animal in exclusion of other reactions. As such, the physiologist need not even touch upon questions involving the intentions, utility, or values of the experimental subject. Such questions, after all, seemed inappropriate for a rigorously scientific theory of human behavior, taking this overly simple model as an earmark of science.

What problems from Merleau-Ponty's point of view are there in the causal chain model as applied to neurology? In Merleau-Ponty's view, problems arise from the fact that stimulus-response theories explain the evidence much in the same way that Ptolemaic theories did. Ptolemaic astronomy could, and in principle still can, explain everything that Newtonian astronomy can. There is no question of finally ruling out one conceptual apparatus over another. At some point however the efforts of the Ptolemaic astronomer to supply more and more *ad hoc* elements, cf. epicycles or eccentricities, begin to make the geocentric theory suspect. In Merleau-Ponty's view, the more sophisticated revisions of the stimulus-response theory, in a similar way, try to save their model by supplementing the original explanatory apparatus with extensive auxiliary hypotheses. They come nearer to the facts only by complicating the original theory as contrary evidence arises.

An example in point arises through Merleau-Ponty's discussion of a condition known as hemianopsia. In this ailment, only the left or right half of each retina functions. Individuals suffering from this condition see at first, as we would expect, one-half of the visual field. (This so far fits with the stimulus-response point of view.) But the whole situation changes, as the subject adjusts to his impairment. The subject then "has the impression of seeing poorly but his vision is not reduced to half of the visual field." (SB, pp. 40–1; SC, pp. 41–2) The eyeballs, in fact, actually oscillate and permit an optimum exposure to the light passing through the lens and the cornea. And, not only does the eyeball as a whole change its position, the functioning of specific neural receptors becomes restructured. The fovea of the retina, when moved to the side through oscillation of the eyeball, loses its property of being particularly sensitive and, a 'pseudo-fovea' arises in what is the center of the retina. One outcome of this condition is that the receptors, which were at the periphery of the retina, actually change their functions.

This restructuring of the retina, in the case of hemianopsia, very much bolsters the importance of conceiving such a condition by use of the notion of Gestalt. Even if we hold that through the action of a "central sector" reflex arcs are reconstituted in such a way that old neural chains are given up and new ones set, we need to know how the "central sector" selects this style of reorganization over another. Issues of preferred behavior are difficult to avoid. If we try to explain the adjustment in the retinas through the stimulus-response format, we are led to presume, by definition, that some neurological circuits are designed to effect a maximization of retinal stimulation. But, this hypothesis does not follow from neurological testing. It only follows from the demands placed upon the stimulus-response theory to account for a transformation in reflex arcs. Furthermore, the introductory auxiliary mechanisms which set out to explain hemianopsia by reflex theory leave out the fact that everything transpires as if the condition is corrected by degrees. The individual's neurology does not finally correct itself by setting the correct new neurological circuits in action. Rather the patient "adjusts" to his condition. Now it is very important to see that such an adjustment would not occur by degree if the patient's neurology could simply recast its circuitry. We have instead what seems to be a way in which the subject reencounters his impaired perception over and over. Shifts are made as perceptual inadequacies are met by new motor responses. In short, the subject's condition changes as a interworking between perception and motoricity are brought into play. We have then a kind of adaptation which fits the Gestalt model, in the third sense of Gestalt (See Merleau-Ponty's use of Gestalt *supra*). The subject is a balance between significations struck by his manner of structuration and the environment in which this effort to maintain such structuration takes place. One cannot speak simply of a stimulus, a reflex arc, and a response, and suppose that this neurological chain operates *partes extra partes*, i. e. as an isolatable part, uninfluenced by the working of other parts, without forgetting the reciprocal interworking of perception and motoricity that takes place in such conditions.

18

2. The three structures of behavior

As I have indicated above, an explanatory theory based on the notion of equilibrium cannot ever hope to falsify a causal theory which depends either on separate events taken in series. It is a question of the efficacy of one model over another. But I would like to note here, at the outset of discussing Merleau-Ponty's three structures of behavior, the "syncretic," the "amovable" and the "symbolic" structures, that just because he speaks of structures instead of causal relations, he is presenting a fresh approach to the great variety of environments that an organism may be open to. If an organism is conceived as a manner of structuration, we have built into the approach the notion that only certain stimuli will be significant for the organism. To take a most primitive case of equilibrium, in a soap bubble, the shape is maintained by the consistency of inner and outer air pressure. But the soap bubble exhibits the same changes in form regardless if the air pressure is increased by an air pump, by a fan, or by the air exhaled by an exuberant political speaker. This simple physical form has an extremely narrow domain of what is admissible for causing change. Organisms are similar in that the field to which the organism responds is itself more or less limited depending on structure. The soap bubble's structure is so simple that a physicalistic explanation is appropriate. Organisms, of course, do not correlate with such a narrowly conceived environment. But it is important to note that the three structures that Merleau-Ponty describes are basically three cases wherein a categorial shift in complexity of structure takes place. This means that from the point of view of the organism, that the organism is in a different environment or world depending upon its structure.

—The Syncretic Form—

The syncretic form is a structural description of instinctual behavior. This kind of behavior can appear to fit the stimulus-response format, insofar as the reactions engendered by the environment on this level are the least flexible. However, the stimulus-response model is still an ill-fitting model here. A single stimulus is not enough to incite instinctual behavior. In this case, a constellation or 'syncresis' is correlated with the animal's activity. An ant, for example, if placed on a stick allows itself to fall on a white paper marked with a black circle only when 1) the circle is a certain size, 2) the distance to the ground is within a given range, 3) the angle of the stick is at a certain inclination, and 4) there is a definite intensity and direction of lighting. (SB, p. 104–5; SC, p. 114–5) In short, the ant requires a constellation of stimuli before it drops from the stick. One stimulus cannot be isolated as the cause; rather the reaction is the product of a very specific concurrence of events, which has a biological value within the natural habitat of the animal. Nevertheless, if the syncresis is arranged purely artificially within the laboratory, where this behavior has no biological value, the animal will behave in the same way. The particular mark of this kind of behavior is that the animal's response is fixed. The ant will engage in the same behavior, regardless of the suitability of its behavior for preserving itself or its species.

—The Amovable Form—

Within this heading falls all the behavior, animal or human, which changes as the animal strikes upon an easier means of attaining a goal. ("Easier" is meant to stand for less pain provoking, less exhausting or more biologically valuable.) Unlike the syncretic form, wherein a certain complex of events is coupled with the same reaction, the mark of this kind of behavior is that the animal exhibits the capacity to adopt new ways of treating the same conditions. Tolman, for example, shows that rats, which can see some food which they habitually attain by a certain path, will all eventually adopt a shorter route, through the happenstance of going down the wrong pathway. (SB, pp. 110–111; SC, pp. 120–121) All the animals revise their means of getting to the food, even though they can see the food from the first pathway, and not the second. The key difference in this kind

20

of behavior is that the structure involved is not organized according to a constellation of events, but an ordering of *significances* which the animal maintains. Thus, whereas we can speak of behavior which appears reflex-like in the case of the syncretic form, in the case of "amovable forms" we have cases of an animal being able to find similar significances within different locations. The net result is that in this second case we have what amounts to habitual behavior, where the notion of habit entails that old *loci* of a habit may be altered and new ones formed.

Merleau-Ponty refers to this structure as "amovable." This odd term is itself revealing. What is important to see is that, although this behavior is flexible in a way that syncretic behavior can never be, there is nonetheless never any indication that the animal sees objects as anything else but a means or a goal. They are signals which mark the way to what the animal wants. As such, movement or change, which demands that we see something within at least two perspectives—that the *same* path which led to the food can later be seen as a blind alley—is not possible for animals in this form. Although amovable behavior is not a reaction locked within a certain situation, it still, once established, casts the significance of situation into a single univocal mold. Ambiguity, in the sense of our ability to find in a single event more than one significance—a key feature of the human order—is, strictly speaking, not possible within this form of behavior.

Again Merleau-Ponty returns to extensive experimental evidence to substantiate his claim. He cites Koehler's work on primates. A chimpanzee will demonstrate the ability to make innumerable alterations in its usual behavior to obtain fruit, but it never manages to obtain the goal if it must at some point, treat the fruit *as something besides a goal* in order to obtain it. If, for example, a piece of fruit is in a box and the chimpanzee can see the fruit in the box, it still never obtains the fruit, as long as the animal must poke at the fruit to open the door to the box. (SB, p. 117; SC, p. 127) This would involve, as Merleau-Ponty points out, seeing the fruit within two perspectives: as a goal and as

21

means to a goal. "The animal," Merleau-Ponty states, "cannot vary the point of view just as it cannot recognize something in different perspectives as the same thing." (SB, p. 118; SC, p. 128)[1] Again, Koehler's descriptions on animal behavior show that a monkey will employ a box to reach a goal hanging overhead. But every indication is that the monkey thereby attributes to the box no other properties than something to touch upon to reach the fruit. The monkey shows extraordinary agility in balancing on the box, yet he never makes an effort to set the box in such a way that it is stable and well based, i. e. a well-built construction for reaching. (SB, p. 115–116; SC, p. 126) This again would involve seeing the box in both the perspective of a balanced construction as well as a stepping stone to a goal. Merleau-Ponty concludes, "what is really lacking in the animal is the symbolic behavior which it would have to possess in order to find an invariant in the external object, under its diversity of aspects . . ." (SB, p. 118; SC, p.128) For the animal, "the object appears clothed with a 'vector,' invested with a functional value which depends upon the effective composition of the field." (SB, p. 116; SC, p. 127) Thus amovable behavior, although more advanced than syncretic behavior, still fails to count as a description of particularly "human" behavior, since objects never have more than a singular reference to a certain biological situation.

—The Symbolic Form—

According to Merleau-Ponty, human beings are the only animals capable of this last form. This is not to say that we maintain ourselves in this form at all times. To do so would involve abandoning the great repertory of our actions which are habitual. In general, animals cannot be pigeon-holed into one category of behavior although we may assign a particular form as "most typical" for a species, as Merleau-Ponty states. (SB, p. 104; SC, p. 114). But, the shift into the "symbolic structure" is accomplished, in Merleau-Ponty's view, only by man.

The mark of symbolic structure of behavior is that a single

22

object has the capacity to take on more than one significance. As such, things are no longer "signals," pointers, as it were, arranged in view of a certain biological task, but "symbols," i. e. entities which permit the ascription of more than one significance or point of view. Merleau-Ponty describes how behavior which responds to things in this way is not found in animals other than man. "A dog," Merleau-Ponty points out, "which is trained to jump up on one chair, then to pass from it to a second chair, will never use—lacking a chair—two stools or a stool and an armchair which is presented to him," (SB, p. 120; SC, pp. 130–131). Such substitutions, however, are a matter of course in symbolic behavior. Given things as "symbols," we freely find in the stool or armchair, alterations from their ordinary use. These objects are not just implements-for-jumping or implements-for-sitting, but indeed *things*, i. e. entities that have their own unity and durability beyond the uses which we impose upon them. As such we strike upon another characteristic of this form of behavior, namely the capacity to improvise. Since, from the beginning, we take our point of view on things to be variable, we are prepared to find new significances in old established ones. The jazz musician who improvises on a melody, can build upon standard progressions and melodic fragments to the extent that he refashions melodies or chord progressions. In so doing, he expresses a basic feature of the symbolic form. Each bit of melody is capable of a transformation in significance. The inherent possibility of alternative significance is, so to speak, "an inheritance" bestowed upon meaning in general within the symbolic form.

This main feature of the symbolic structure, i. e. its inclusion of an ambiguity of significances ought not to be underestimated. The consequences are vast. Since we are open to a field of action where any thing is more than its momentary appearance, we have not only an environment (*Umwelt*), but a world (*Welt*),[2] Consequently among many other fundamental structural differences, we have the possibility of de-centralizing our own existence. Hence self-knowledge, as a perception of one's own view on things is possible. Also since the capacity to see alternative significances allows one to envision something beyond one's own possibilities and projects, we are confronted with limits to our perspectives which includes an acknowledgement of the possibility of one's own death.

Symbolic behavior also creates a world where a thing can be taken as indeterminate. Suppose, for example, I break open a large piece of marble with a hammer. I see the particular patterns made by the crystalline fissures. But at the same time I understand this is only one aspect of the stone. I know that the rock may be cut in many other ways. The possibilities of its exploration are not limited by one view or another; even so I know these possibilities are "there," in the rock. Thus one can find in Merleau-Ponty's symbolic form a Gestaltist version of Husserl's notions of interior or exterior horizons. And certainly it is part of Merleau-Ponty's concern in *The Structure of Behavior* to broaden the notion of Gestalt so that features of Husserl's phenomenological researches can be seen within a structural format. He tells us in a note that "The notion of intentionality will be helpful in this regard." (SB, p. 249; SC, p. 237). In so saying he is implying that the relationship between intentionality and profiles of things should be conceived as a "lived relation" i. e. a structural relation in his sense of a symbolic structure as Gestalt. (SB, p. 220; SC, p. 236–237).

3. The physical, vital and human orders and Merleau-Ponty's first answer to the mind/body problem

"No form has its sufficient cause outside of itself," Merleau-Ponty tells us in his introduction to his section on the "Physical, Vital and Human Orders." (SB p. 134; SC p. 144) In this phrase, Merleau-Ponty notes the thought which leads him to see in the structures he has described a way of rectifying a collection of confusions. We may consider various orders of things: physical objects, living beings, and notions connected with our mental life. In accordance with these groups, we may discuss a "physical order" a "vital order" and a "human order." Because of our tendency to make one of these orders into the primary

24

reality, an *omnitudo realitatis*, we encounter a host of problems. One needs to think the phrase, "no form has sufficient cause outside of itself" in its consequences to see Merleau-Ponty's way out of these problems which include confusions associated with the relationship of mind to body.

Merleau-Ponty's intent in discussing The Physical Order is to show that explaining physical events by laws and theories which account for facts already is muddled with matter versus idea confusions. For Merleau-Ponty, in *The Structure of Behavior* both conceptual problems as well as ontological problems are resolved if one rethinks physical explanation in terms of Gestalt. Consider. for example, the law of falling bodies. In order to speak of a relationship between a body and its speed in falling, many factors must be ruled out as irrelevant. We need to presume that the centrifugal force of the earth's rotation is constant. We need to consider as irrelevant the gravitational attraction of the moon and for that matter all other celestial bodies. (The speed of the falling body would result in a different equation if a large star neared our solar system.) In short, the law of falling bodies which purports to be an exact account of the movement of all bodies with regards to gravitational pull and time, is actually an idealization of a multitude of factors, none of which are independent from other parts of the system. In other words, we have again events which, if the full picture is admitted, require a model involving a dialectical arrangement between a great variety of forces. The full list of these forces is, in principle, indeterminate. (In the case of gravity, for example, we cannot specify all grivitional forces brought about by the multitude of galaxies.)

An application of the notion of Gestalt to physical explanation had already been offered by Gestaltists such as Koffka in his *Principles of Gestalt Psychology*. But as Merleau-Ponty points out, the ramifications of the notion of Gestalt were not conceived of even by this founder of the Gestalt school. Koffka writes:

I admit that in our *ultimate* explanations, we can have but *one* universe of discourse and that it must be the one about which physics has taught us so much. (quoted in SB p. 133, SC p. 144)

In effect, Koffka is holding that the physical world is the real world and that explanations finally must address it. But is he thinking rigorously in terms of the consequences of his own notion of Gestalt? A Gestalt, as a form, is given its meaning by the interplay of interior and exterior forces. Finally to say that one kind of Gestalt involves an order more real than any other is simply to indicate a preference in terms of one manner of meaning over another. Thinking matters further, one needs to hold, as Merleau-Ponty claims, that the occasion for finding a particularly Gestalt meaningful is dependent itself upon a dialectical movement in which form or structure is discovered. Or in other words, one needs to hold that the Gestalt which fits physical explanations itself has a "geneology." It has been attained through processes of discovery, reconsideration, testing, fitting, correction, etc., which are themselves in each case manners of behavior within, what he calls, the "human order." As, he states, (SB, p. 142; SC, 153) "Form is not an element of the world but a limit toward which physical knowledge tends and which it itself defines." The expressions "limit" and "tends" should be stressed in this quote. These terms indicate Merleau-Ponty's consistent application in *Structure of Behavior* of the notion of Gestalt in the third sense indicated at the beginning of this chapter. Physical knowledge "tends" toward a Gestalt insofar as we are directed towards a world; it is a "limit" insofar as physical knowledge leads us to a Gestalt which is a terminus for explaining the world. But, there is no reason to hold that any such Gestalt has "a sufficient cause outside of itself." In other words there is no reason to hold that the physical order, which is itself constructed from the human order, is an *omnitudo realitatis*. This is Koffka's error.

The direction of Merleau-Ponty's thought in relationship to "the vital order" is similar to the discussion of the physical order. Historically, biologists have spoken of an "entelechy," an "*elan vitale*" or even a "final cause," or, in general, of "life." These classical concepts, as well as theories which involve the positing of instincts or drives presume an internal cause for the animal's behavior, which explains how an animal prefers one sort of object over another. But we are again led either into the problem of inquiries which would set the animal in a world of physical objects as defined by our own common sense account of physical objects, or into an inquiry in regards to the manner of intelligence the animal may be exhibiting in choosing among such objects. Such inquiries are two sides of the same error. As shown through the discussion of syncretic and amovable forms, an animal's behavior expresses a Gestalt which exhibits a "unity of signification" (SB p. 156; SC p. 169). It is not open to our world, whether it is conceived as the world of common sense objects, or of transcendental categories. The animal's own structural orientation admits a restricted dialectic. Again, the animal's structural orientation admits "no sufficient cause outside of itself." Explaining the animal's behavior in terms of physical objects imposes the meaning of one Gestalt upon another. As Merleau-Ponty states in explaining how relevant considerations are brought into explaining the behavior of an insect:

> A purely objective method can delineate the structure of the "colors" in butterflies by comparing the reactions which are evoked in them by the different colored stimuli—precisely on the condition of limiting oneself strictly to the identity of difference of the responses in the presence of such and such given stimuli and of not projecting our living experience of colors into the butterfly's consciousness. (SB, p. 183; SC, p. 197)

In other words, what counts as an "objective method" in explaining the vital order depends upon a matching of the animals behavior with its perception. The interplay between the two expresses the animal's environment. Adding our own perspective may be conceived as a "projection" of our experience of colors, etc.

We come then to Merleau-Ponty's account of "the human order" He states:

> What defines man is not the capacity to create a second nature—
> economic, social or cultural—beyond biological nature; it is rather the

capacity of going beyond created structures in order to create others. And this movement is already visible in each of the particular products of human work. (SB, p. 175; SC, p. 189)

The defining feature of the human order in Merleau-Ponty's view may be approached along the lines of a theory of meaning. To cite a key notion which is initiated in *The Structure of Behavior* but which is examined in much more detail in *The Phenomenology of Perception*, for human beings meaning can be "ambiguous." And in particularly human activities, meaning always is ambiguous. (See SB, p. 176; SC, p. 190 for his introduction of this sense of ambiguity.) By ambiguity, Merleau Ponty implies here not the notion of a equivocation, worse yet, vagueness or fuzziness, but that for human beings, who are operating in "the human order," the meaning given to an action, expression, or perception, always remains capable of additional interpretations. This open-endedness of meaning allows for the improvisation of one structure upon another, since meaning in the human order although provisionally circumscribable, is never fully fixed and determined. The quote which heads the beginning of this chapter, where El Greco's visual anomaly is said to "receive a universal signification by the mediation of the artist" is an example in point. El Greco's human figures, in their manners of elongation express both a vulnerability and strength. El Greco is not operating solely in the physical or vital orders. It is not only a visual anomaly which his elongated figures express. Nor can we speak, with adequate explanation, of the biological goals which his paintings provide. No, rather, his figures are ambiguous in Merleau-Ponty's sense. They open outward to a meaning which is more than he could count on by setting himself upon a fixed meaning or significance. His astigmatism becomes the occasion of expressing aspects of the human condition. In his anomaly he exposes and emphasizes the endurance of the human figure and perhaps, if one will overlook the puns, reveals a fundamental human longing for what is upright and just. In short it is El Greco's genius to broaden neurological accidents even to the point of metaphysics.

Turning to more mundane examples, take, for example, clothing, food, and shelter. Only men, so the saying goes, understand themselves to be naked. We may grant of course, that children of an early age have little sense of nakedness and different cultures admit all sorts of different versions of what clothing determines "being dressed" and which does not. But the question is not one of noting the cultural significance of clothing in various cultures. Rather it is a question of what is presumed in order for clothing to take on such a array of different significances. Merleau-Ponty's point is that clothing, as is the case with every particularly human artifact, expresses the human order, just because clothing comes ready with the capacity to express more than a singular significance. Thus it can be a means for adornment, or competition, or statement of social relations. In the middle ages Sumptuary Laws prescribed the clothing which specific classes were required to wear. We no longer hold to such a classification. We need to ask what sort of thing clothing is that it would admit such a cultural practice, while being at the same time a use-object designed to protect us from cold. In so asking we come to the inherent "ambiguity" of this article in the Merleau-Pontean sense. We may observe similar "ambiguity" in the case of food and shelter. To supply an account of these articles in terms of their vital significance alone, would be to confuse one manner of Gestalt with another. This is precisely what is accomplished when human behavior is reduced to drives or instincts which are defined as directed to a goal.

We may now consider Merleau-Ponty's account of the mind/body relation. In a note he quotes part of Proust's description of his grandmother's death in *Le Côté des Guermantes*:

> . . . her hand which threw off the covers with a gesture which had at another time signified that they had annoyed her and which now signified nothing. (SB p. 249; SC p. 226)

Proust's description indicates a shift from the human gestures of throwing off bed covers—itself an expression of a human action—to the same action, which given the death of Marcel's grandmother, "signified nothing." This lack of meaning is a lack of human meaning. The action of her limbs became mechanical and meaningless. In Merleau-Ponty's understanding, this absence of meaning, which occurs when the old woman dies, indicates an absence of meaning only because the human order can no longer be maintained. There is movement nonetheless; but it is movement which entails a disintegration of a highly complex Gestalt, described by the symbolic structure, into mere physical Gestalt which gives the old woman's action neither a vital nor a human significance.

Problems of the relationship of the body to the mind are engendered by the fact that an organism can integrate itself along the lines of more sophisticated Gestalts. To the extent that the integration is partial—and this will always be the case to varying degrees—one will speak loosely of a distinction between the body and the mind. And we should add that these terms, insofar as they imply that there is some *thing* which they refer to, hide the fact that the relationship between the body and the mind is dialectical, always admitting various manners of integration. Merleau-Ponty describes this "dialectical" relationship which expresses the mind-body relation as follows:

> There is always a duality which reappears at one level or another: hunger or thirst prevents thought or feelings; the properly sexual dialectic ordinarily reveals itself through a passion; integration is never absolute and always fails—at a high level in the writer, at a lower level in the aphasic. There always comes a moment when we divest ourselves of a passion because of fatigue or self-respect. This duality is not a simple fact; it is founded in principle—all integration presupposing the normal functioning of subordinated formations, which always demand there own due. (SB p. 210; SC p. 226–227)

As Merleau-Ponty indicates in another passage, "The relation of each order to the higher order is that of the partial to the total. . . . The advent of higher orders to the extent that they are accomplished, eliminate the autonomy of the lower order and give signification to the steps which constitute them. That is why we have spoken of a human rather than of a mental or a rational order." (SB, p. 180; SC, p. 195)[3] Thus the notion of Gestalt in the sense of the accomplishment of more complex Gestalts is accountable for the apparent differences between mind and body relationships.

Let us look at some concrete cases which indicate how we are to see Merleau-Ponty's theory of mind-body relations. Consider the case of an individual with an extreme lacking of integration in the "higher" orders. For a patient in a coma, for example, it may be possible to explain patterns of breathing strictly by their vital significance. But breathing is a function which admits considerable shifts from vital significance to human significance. Someone may use breathing—a sigh—to express exasperation. A mathematician's breathing may begin to quicken because of the anticipation of discovering a proof. In the first case, the patient in a coma, we are speaking of breathing which is only, as we say, "a vital sign." But in the case of the person who breathes a sigh to express exasperation, although he is fulfilling his need for oxygen, his breathing is also expressive of his human situation. What in other contexts might be called mind seems to be at work in this apparent case of vital functioning. But from Merleau-Ponty's point of view, to suppose that mind is now controlling the body, in some manner, is to engage again in a confusion of the Gestalts associated with the three orders. Once Gestalt again is made into a "sufficient cause" of another. In this case the mind, which in fact may be variously interpreted as being in the vital or human order, is made into the cause of his respiration. But besides affording a conceptual muddle, holding that our mind controls such a vital function does not fit our experience. In Merleau-Ponty's view, the question of cause between orders ought not to arise. We have instead simply an integration to a higher order. The man's breathing expresses his exasperation because his body is to a larger extent in the human order. As such breathing is included within the gestures associated with inter-human relations.

Once one is speaking of an individual largely operating within the human order, much greater scope is given to where we would say the mind extends or where the body begins. If we imagine, for example, a committed statesman speaking against a surprise military attack, we may say that intelligence pervades his whole body. We cannot say his mind is simply behind his face and his body is a kind of chemical factory which supports it. We see his indignation and his intentions in his body from head to toe. Again, it does not fit to say his mind is like a puppeteer pulling the strings of his body. To cite the classical analogies, his mind is not in his body like the pilot in his ship or like the artisan working his tools. Protesting the military invasion, we might see his body slump, hear his voice break, etc. In such cases of dedication, extreme commitment or passion, the body becomes largely incorporated into the intentions of the individual. It would be curious indeed to suppose that the statesman we have described, if he is sincere, willed his body to represent the meaning of the military invasion. Such a preparing of the body is unnecessary; in such cases of intense commitment, which by definition entails a subordinating of one's life to a human enterprise, one *is* one's body.

What of occasions then when the body is said to act upon the mind? Literature is filled with descriptions where intelligent and prudent behavior is overthrown by physical need. Phraedra is pulled by a sexual passion for her step-son and her longing, it is quite clear, is quite alien to her plans. In Merleau-Ponty's terms, her nurse, in the Euripidean version, possesses the integration, she lacks. It is not possible for her to consider attempting to seduce Hippolytus or even to tolerate her passion, as her nurse would have her do. Such a passion does not have a place within her world. But her world, her "human order," may collapse.[4] Her sexual desire can overpower the manner in which she may fittingly ascribe significance. As such she may "lose her mind" or be "beside herself." But in both cases what fits into the common locution of "mind" or "self" here is the extent and manner to which vital significances have been given human significance. In both cases, one has a shift in the manner of meaning which the concept of self and mind in various ways— and with various confusions—touch upon.

32

As Merleau-Ponty points out, the notion of mind imposes the notion of a *de facto* order of mind (SB p. 180; SC p. 195). In most theories it is taken to be a notion which is at least cognizant of linguistic significance. But it often permits a conceptualization which, by definition, is restrictive of the body. This is true in the tradition of which Descartes is taken to be the founder. The problem henceforth lies not in the apparent dichotomy of mind-body, but in the narrow meaning allotted to mental life. What is problematic is a conception of mind which operates in a realm of strictly delineated scope and not in a realm of possibility. It is in this sense that mind is given, as Merleau-Ponty claims, the significance of a *de facto* order. Once such an order is presumed, mind-body relations become a problem. The Cartesian concept of mind presumes a theory of meaning which entails that meaning does not admit ambiguity—that meaning does not entail, even in its expression, the possibility of further interpretations. Mental life in the posing of the problem is characterized as exclusive of physical life. This narrow concept of mind is so established that the term itself cannot be used without engendering muddles. Hence, Merleau-Ponty's choice to speak of a human order and not mental one. His notion of the human order allows him to account for what appears to be the submergence or emergence of mind in relationship to the body and how in ordinary activities the two appear for the most part interdependent.

4. Gestalt and intentionality are implicitly reconceived

At the outset of this chapter, I pointed out that Merleau-Ponty tends to couch his own views, particularly in his early work, in the formulations of other thinkers. In his discussion of the "human order," we see this manner of presentation. In discussing the "human order," he finally offers a conception of human being which suggests elements of Husserl's theory of intentionality as well as Gestalt theory. The following two quotes express these influences.

Rather, consciousness is a network of significative intentions which are sometimes clear to themselves and sometimes on the contrary, lived rather than known. Such a conception will permit us to link consciousness with action by enlarging our idea of action. (SB p. 173; SC p. 187)

Man can never be an animal: his life is always more or less integrated than that of an animal. But if the alleged instincts of man do not exist *apart* from the mental dialectic, correlatively, this dialectic is not conceivable outside of the concrete situations in which it is embedded. One does not act with the mind alone. Either mind is nothing or it constitutes a real and not an ideal transformation of man. Because it is not a new sort of being but a new form of unity, it cannot stand by itself. (SB, p. 181; SC, p. 196)

What Merleau-Ponty finally prepares for us in his discussion of human order is a view which presents an account of the intentional view of consciousness as in a dialectical relationship with "nature," where nature simply implies that which we are directed toward in the world. But, this dialectical relationship, insofar as it is part of the human order, permits the accretion of significances which are, in principle, not complete. Thus we may address issues or areas of the world towards which a fixed object is not intended. Now I suggest that although the notion of form has served its purpose in allowing Merleau-Ponty to readdress the issue of intentionality, he has in fact expanded its usages to the extent that the notion of Gestalt and intention have been recast.

Merleau-Ponty is led to say on the last page of *The Structure of Behavior* "If we understand by perception the act which makes us know existences, all the problems which we have touched upon are reducible to the problem of perception." (SB, p. 224; SB, p. 240). His logic here, I believe, is quite consistent. If you accept the view that various manners of explanation are cases of the expression of different sorts of Gestalt, and if you accept also that a Gestalt is something which is struck upon within the human order, then an understanding of the human order prepares an understanding of explanatory theory in general. Add to this as well, that the human order, itself, is a dialectical relationship between the way we are directed towards the world and the manner in which the world presents significances for us. We have then the the the view he has come to: the key locus of such a human/world interchange is to be found in perception. It is in perception that the human/world interchange directly takes place. Hence Merleau-Ponty's direction in his second work, *The Phenomenology of Perception*. But what is left out in this conclusion, is that he has prepared an account of the human world already for which both the issues of consciousness as described by Husserl or Gestalt as described by the Gestaltists are inadequate.

In discussing the "ambiguity" of the human order Merleau-Ponty is not proposing the view, as does Husserl that meaning is to be thought of as a subject/object relationship. Quite the contrary. It is in the nature of both the intentional act and the intentional object that—if one may use such terms in relationship to Merleau-Ponty's views—there is ambiguity. As he states repeatedly, "the human dialectic involves the capacity of orienting oneself to "the possible." (SB, p. 176; SC, p. 190) This means that intentionality can neither be properly spoken of as a specific act or object. Furthermore, Husserlian analyses presume, even in the expression of "operative intentionality" that meaning is an *Erfüllung* relationship. Meaning is given or "filled in" by the intentional subject.[6] Husserl's writings are in fact dominated by the model of a filling in. Even in his later works where he speaks of the indeterminate, he sees the indeterminate as the "empty"[7] and says that determination is equivalent to the "correction" of the indeterminate.[8] But this is far from Merleau-Ponty's view. His arrival at the importance of perception is dependent upon the notion that in perception the human/world dialectic takes place. In general the notion of structure which, as we have seen, is a primary theme throughout *The Structure of Behavior* is alien to Husserl's view that a subject constitutes the meaning he finds in the world.

But it is also true to say that Merleau-Ponty has altered the notion of Gestalt as it is used by Gestalt psychology. Merleau-Ponty ascribes to the view of Gestaltists, such as Kohler, Kaffka and Wertheimer, that a Gestalt gets its significance through the equilibrium established between interior and exterior parts. But in presenting his view of the human world Merleau-Ponty offers what might be called a "world-Gestalt." Here the theory of meaning which he ascribes to the human order admits scarce relation to Gestalt theorists. The human/world interchange described in the human order is a "vertical dialectic." That is to say, because of the inherent ambiguity both in human actions and perceptions, earlier significances are both preserved and overcome as new meanings are cast upon the old. But Merleau-Ponty's interest in the notion of Gestalt has rested to large extent in the capacity of Gestalt to be "in" things. The Gestalt expresses the animal's behavior. Theory and fact are not separated. In the case of amovable structures, for example, we are speaking of a Gestalt which appears *in* and *as* the environment of the animal. We have a different situation with the human order. No contours or shaping can be drawn, even in the sense of significances. As a vertical dialectic, form has become, in principle, amorphous. This feature of the human order, in my opinion, strains to the breaking point the Gestaltist's sense of the notion of Gestalt. It is not that it serves no purpose. As we have shown, it enables Merleau-Ponty to handle mind-body problems as well as set up an inquiry into what needs to be accepted or rejected in Husserl's phenomenology. But, the notion of Gestalt as Merleau-Ponty finally uses it in the human form simply does not admit the usual language which goes with the term, such as equilibrium, whole and part. In Merleau-Ponty's notion of the human order, the Gestalt involved is in a sense always out of equilibrium since the possibility of a new cast of signification is entailed in its most basic instances. Nor can one ever speak of the boundaries or limits of the whole, as one can with the vital order. At the risk of verbal play, one might say in Merleau-Ponty's transformed usage of Gestalt, the part is always greater than the whole, since any aspect of our world may extend itself beyond what we take the world as some point to be. What Merleau-Ponty finally leaves us with in his concept of Gestalt is the notion of dialectic or a way in which we are conversant with the world. This manner of dialectic brings home, in a way that

Husserlian intentionality does not, that our position is always contingent upon our interchange with the world. And in particular, his view in *The Structure of Behavior* shows how our human world may disintegrate into the physical or vital orders should our humanity be overcome. The ramifications of Merleau-Ponty's view continue to be hampered by his respecting the doctrine of intentionality, even in his implicit revisions, throughout the whole of *The Phenomenology of Perception*. Of course his account of the body-subject is a crucial contribution. But as far as his full working out of the consequences of his understanding of the human order, he does not fully follow the lead of his own thought until *The Visible and the Invisible*.

Notes to Chapter One

[1] The notion of perspective implies an alternate point of view. Various aspects of the multi-perspectival aspect of particularly human activities have been described by many authors. Arthur Koestler, in *The Act of Creation*, London, Hutchinson, 1976, argues that irony and humor, among other particularly human phenomena, have a structure he calls "bisociative." These expressions, for Koestler, involve seeing something from two perspectives at once. This amounts to a special case of Merleau-Ponty's notion of ambiguity.

[2] Merleau-Ponty seems heavily influenced, at this point, by Scheler's account of man's 'world-openness.' Passages like the following indicate the force of Scheler's thought: "The animal has no 'object'. It lives, as it were, ecstatically immersed in its environment which it carries along as a snail carries its shell. It cannot perform the peculiar act of detachment and distance by which man transforms an 'enviroment' (*Umwelt*) into the 'world' (*Welt*), or into a symbol of the world. It cannot perform that act by which man transforms the centers of resistance determined by drives and affects into 'objects.' " Scheler, *Man's Place in Nature*, Noonday Press, New York, Meyerhoff translation, p. 39. It is influences like Scheler's, himself a student of Husserl's, which undermine the intellectual narrative format. It is quite possible that Scheler helped to build part of the context in which Merleau-Ponty read Husserl and Heidegger. But then again, perhaps it is the other way around. Indeed, these questions ought not to be posed if one expects an answer which would see the development of a philosopher as the result of a series of influences.

[3] The quote without ellipses runs as follows: "The relation of each order to the higher order is that of the partial to the total. A normal man is not a body bearing autonomous instincts joined to a 'psychological life' defined by certain characteristic processes—pleasure and pain, emotion, association of ideas—and surmounted with a mind which would enfold its proper acts over this infrastructure. The advent of higher orders, to the extent that they are accomplished, eliminate the autonomy of the lower orders and give new signification to the step which constitute them. This is why we have spoken of a

human order rather than a mental or rational order. The so frequent distinction of the mental and the somatic has its place in pathology but cannot serve for the knowledge of the normal man, since in him the somatic processes do not unfold in isolation but are integrated into a cycle of more extensive action. It is not a question of two *de facto* orders external to each other, but two types of relations, the second which integrates the first." (SB, p. 180; SC p. 195)

4 For Merleau-Ponty's discussion of the disintegration of structures see SB, pp. 176–184, 202–4; SC 191–199, 220–222. He states for example: (SB, p. 204; SC, p. 220) "For a being who has acquired consciousness of self and his body, who has reached the dialectic of subject and object, the body is no longer the cause of the structure of consciousness; it has become an object of consciousness. Then one can no longer speak of a psycho-physiological parallelism: only a disintegrated consciousness can be paralleled with physiological processes, that is with a partial functioning of the organism."

5 Paul D. Maclean in "The Paranoid Streak in Man" in *Beyond Reductionism* edited by Arthur Koestler and J. R. Smythies (Boston, Beacon Press, 1969), presents a physiological account of the brain which accords remarkably with the tripart division of structures proposed by Merleau-Ponty. In Maclean's view, the human brain, in its structure, contains an "ancient part" still physiologically similar to primitive developments. This part he dubs the "reptilian brain." Encircling it is the old mammalian brain, consisting of the limbic system. Last the neo-cortex which is highly developed in primates and most especially so in *homo sapiens*. The reptilian brain is concerned with behavior which is least susceptible to adaptation. The limbic cortex on the other hand is not so highly tied to specific stimuli and includes behavior such as searching and protecting. The neo-cortex is responsible, to speak most generally for, among other kinds of behavior, "voluntary movement" and linguistic usage. MacLean's view is intriguing from the perspective of Merleau-Ponty's theories of the structures of behavior in that, the neo-cortex is taken to be flexible in regards to how various main anatomical sites may be functioning. MacLean proposes from a physiological point of view a question which is similar to Merleau-Ponty's inquiry into mind-body relations. The human brain is given the problem, so to speak, of integrating its three main developments. It does so in varying degrees of successfulness. Full integration into neo-cortex functionings is never wholly accomplished. But the brain may function in varying degrees of discontinuity or integration of "reptilian" versus "mammalian" or "symbolic" brands of behavior.

6 In an article by Fink of which Husserl himself stated: "I have carefully read through this essay at the request of the able editors of the *Kant-Studien* and I am happy to state that it contains no sentence which I could not completely accept as my own or openly acknowledge as my own conviction," we find Fink writing the following: "The phenomenological reduction is not primarily a method of simply 'disconnecting,' but one of *leading back*. It leads, through the most extreme radicalism of self-reflection, the philosophizing subject *back through itself* to the transcendental life of belief (a life which is concealed by the subject's human self-apperception) whose acceptance-correlate the world "*is*." (Fink's emphasis, p. 126) In my opinion, this essay which reflects Husserl's later views, clearly indicates that Husserl meant to uphold his earlier notion that our world is the construct of a transcendental subject. As such the dialectical relation of man/world that Merleau-Ponty endeavors to clarify is quite alien to Husserl's thought. Fink's article with Husserl's preface is reprinted and translated in Elveton, R. O., *The Phenomenology of Husserl*, Quadrangle Books, Chicago, 1970, pp. 73–147.

[7] See Husserl's, *Experience and Judgement*. Revised and edited by Landgrebe, Northwestern University Press, 1973, Evanston, Illinois, pp. 125 ff.

[8] See Husserl's, *The Crisis of the European Sciences and Transcendental Phenomenology*, translated by David Carr, Northwestern University Press, 1970, Evanston, Illinois, p. 163.

2

The Phenomenology of Perception— The Body-Subject and its Pact with the Natural World

Mes repentirs, mes doutes, mes contraintes
Sont le défaut de ton grand diamant . . .

My doubts, my strivings, my repentances,
These are the flaw in your great diamond . . .
                        Paul Valéry, *Le Cimetière marin*

What we have said at the start . . . makes of my incarnation no longers
a "difficulty," a fault in the clear diamond of philosophy—but the typical
fact . . . (VI p. 233; *VI* p. 287)

1. In Place of the Flawed Diamond

I have chosen the title, *In Place of the Flawed Diamond* having in mind Heidegger's notion of a saying as a "way-making."[1] Merleau-Ponty characterizes the perceptual world and finally the concept of philosophy which he means to correct as *a flawed diamond*. He offers his own philosophy in place of this approach. Perhaps, in a book of explication, a metaphor, such as this one, which has the capacity to lead our thought to distinctions not yet made, may serve as a "way-making" in the Heideggerian sense.

The metaphor of a "flawed diamond" actually occurs at the beginning of the chapter entitled "le Sentir" in *The Phenomenology of Perception*. Here Merleau-Ponty in turn alludes to Valéry's *Le Cimetière marin*. Why a flawed diamond? The figure sketches Merleau-Ponty's approach in various ways. In the context of Merleau-Ponty's book, "the flawed diamond" suggests the error of holding that there are isolatable, immutable, "atoms" of perceptual experience. The "great diamond" referred to in Valéry's poem, also suggests a world unchanging in time. As we shall see, the world Merleau-Ponty finally describes appears only through temporal interrelationships. An immutable world would in fact exclude perceptual experience. So the great diamond is unavoidably flawed. Furthermore, for Merleau-Ponty, philosophy does not succeed if it attempts to offer a fixed conceptual apparatus for describing our world. Merleau-Ponty means to undo the notion that the perceptual world is made up of data which are context-free—undo both the notion that there is data free from relation to fields as well as the notion that there are fields free from relations to other fields. And, he holds that both our perceptual and cognitive life is founded upon a mutable subject, the "lived body." In his last work *The Visible and the Invisible* he extends his criticism of "the great diamond" further. He holds that primary philosophical distinctions are to be corrected insofar as they would involve *positive signification* altogether. The criticism of context-free, isolatable data is extended finally to errors in the manner of making primary distinctions as context-independent. Perhaps then the phrase, *in place of the flawed diamond*, might serve as a "way-making" in that it can help to introduce an opening for the thought that Merleau-Ponty is directing us toward.

In this chapter our primary concern will be an investigation of Merleau-Ponty's notion of the body which I will also refer to as the *body-subject*. In *The Phenomenology of Perception*, the theory of the body is approached by an examination of *le prèjugé du monde*, that is a prejudice in favor of the objective world. I will follow his approach in this explication. In Merleau-Ponty's view, the *prèjugé du monde* is part of the cultural acquisition of the European tradition and is expressed by epistemologists representing both empiricist and rationalist schools. For the sake of putting Merleau-Ponty's notion of *le prèjugé du monde* further into historical perspective, I will also pose a comparison between *le prèjugé du monde* and Heidegger's account of

42

traditional errors in the ontology of a thing as he presents them in *The Origin of the Work of Art*. Heidegger's account of "the thing" in fact complements Merleau-Ponty's views on traditional prejudices.

2. The "thingliness" of the thing: Heidegger's account and its similarity to Merleau-Ponty's

The interpretations of the thingness of the thing which, predominant in the course of Western thought, have long become self-evident and are now in everyday use, may be reduced to three.

Heidegger, *The Origin of the Work of Art*[2]

In *The Origin of the Work of Art*, Heidegger takes up an issue which appears often in his writings: traditions according to which "the thing" has been conceived in Western thought. In this essay he offers an overview of three basic traditions, all from his point of view, in error. I must recommend this essay to those who wish to profit in full from his analyses. I will offer a synopsis here of Heidegger's view. I believe that it contributes to Merleau-Ponty's thought in that both thinkers are uncovering ontological errors which are rooted in our culture and which make theories which are ontologically revisionary, such as Merleau-Ponty's theory of the body, difficult to comprehend.

In Heidegger's understanding, a first concept of a thing arises near the origins of our philosophic tradition when several ways of naming a thing, as spoken in Greek, came to be translated into Latin. Through a collation of grammar and ontology, a tradition arose from Latin writers whereby a thing was taken to be a substance that possessed attributes or properties. This ontology was supported by the subject/predicate grammatical relation. Heidegger states:[3]

. . . this first interpretation of the thingness of the thing, the thing as bearer of its characteristic traits, despite it currency, is not as natural as it appears to be. What seems natural to us is probably Just something familiar in a long tradition that has forgotten the unfamiliar source from which it arose.

Early in the introductory chapter, Merleau-Ponty describes a "red patch"—a description which is developed from Sartre's *L'Imaginaire*.

> This red patch which I see on the carpet is red only in virtue of a shadow which lies across it, its quality is apparent only in relationship to the play of light upon it, and hence as an element of spatial configuration. Moreover the colour can be said to be there only if it occupies an area of a certain size, too small an area not being describable in these terms. Finally this red would literally not be the same if it were not the 'woolly red' of a carpet. (Ph.P, p. 4; PP. p. 10)

Merleau-Ponty's description above details the faults of Heidegger's first ontology. Seeing things according to the substance/attribute ontology leads us to think that just as predicates are true or false of a subject, qualities are truly or falsely possessed by a substance. We are led to accept a model of a thing where it contains, possesses, organizes or collects various qualities. From Merleau-Ponty's view a great disservice is being done to our actual perception through this model. There is a logic to the perceptual field in which all the senses as well as the body's motoricity interplay. As he states, the space of a symphony hall shifts as the musicians begin to perform.

> Music is not in visible space, but it beseiges, undermines and displaces that space . . . (Ph.P, p. 225; PP p. 260)

Sound, no less than a logic of color, size, bodily motority, etc. plays into our overall perception of the perceptual field.

Let us consider his remarks about the red patch cited above. He says: ". . . the carpet is red only in virtue of a shadow which lies across it, its quality is apparent only in relation to the play of light upon it, and hence as an element of spatial configuration." Consider the notion of spatial configuration as it appears in this passage. A color, such as "this red patch" is perceived partly with reference to its shadow. It is not solely contained in a substance. If tested by a spectograph the same red patch will give a different hue reading depending upon whether it is tested

44

in exterior lighting, in indoor incandescent lighting or in indoor phosphorescent lighting. What sense is there in saying that the same quality of red is predicable of the carpet? From Merleau-Ponty's point of view its sameness is a feature of our capacity to reorder perceptual differences as we relocate the color spectrum. We find the logic of the spectrum in a new setting. Photographers often experience how the color spectrum returns as they pass from ordinary incandescent lighting to the red light of a dark room. According to a spectograph the hues of the colors in the dark room are all reddish. Nonetheless, the photographer finds again the "true" colors as he adjusts to the unnatural lighting. This logic of the color spectrum, rediscovered as illumination changes, has little to do with patches which *in themselves* are a particular hue. Rather as Merleau-Ponty chooses often to say, it is a question of the *sens* of the perception. He plays here upon a feature of the French language which contains in the word *sens* both notions of "sense" and "direction." Each quality is *directed* by the overall logic of the perceptual field. Thus in the example quoted above, the shadow is taken into account in our seeing the red patch. But then the substance/attribute model does an injustice to our perception. It removes us from the network and interworking of colors, sounds, tactile phenomena, etc. in the perceptual field as a whole.

A second problem with the substance/attribute model is that some attributes do not adhere to any substance. We may consider the quote above again to this purpose. Merleau-Ponty mentions that "the colour is said to be part of a thing only if it occupies an area of a certain size." If there is a color so pervasive as to count as thematic to a whole spectacle, as in the case of artists who investigate a shade of pink or blue making it thematic to works of a certain period, cf. Picasso's Blue Period, the color solicits an overall mood for the painting. Such thematic colors are not colors (attributes) of objects. Thus size itself not only shifts the character of an color, it can remove it from having relevance to some specific object altogether. The notion of color qualities, not bound to some object, having atmospheric value, is clearly not one we would expect given the substance/attribute ontology.

A second tradition whereby we come to understand a thing, according to Heidegger's historiography of the thing, is a reaction to the older substance/attribute dichotomy. According to his view:

"Occasionally we still have the feeling that violence has been done to the thingly element of things and that thought has played its part in that violence, for which people disavow thought instead of taking pains to make it more thoughtful."[4]

This second tradition which endeavors to overcome the violence done to the thing "without taking pains to be more thoughtful" sees the thing as a "sensible." It is a collection of sensations of color, sound, roughness and hardness, etc. Historically, this tradition arises at the same time as the invention of the field of Aesthetics which would treat the art object along lines of *aisthesis*, that is along the lines of a theory of sensation. The world or language which stands as a background to the artwork is lost in the process and so a great detour with grave consequences was made in the formulation of the subject matter of Aesthetics. In terms of theories of perception, the view is not so much wrong as it forgets the original goal. How do we account for our seeing, hearing, etc. of a *thing*? The itemization of sensations will never add up to the thing. In Heidegger's view:

We never really first perceive a throng of sensations, e. g. tones and noises, in the appearance of things—as this thing concept alleges: rather we hear the storm whistling in the chimney, we hear the three-motored plane, we hear the Mercedes in immediate distinction from the Volkswagon.[5]

Merleau-Ponty's view parallels Heidegger's. As he states:

46

... it is impossible completely to describe the colour of the carpet without saying that it *is* a carpet, made of wool and without implying that in this color a certain tactile value, a certain weight and a certain resistance to sound. (Ph.P, p. 323; PP. p. 373)

An example which illustrates this point is offered by Hubert Dreyfus in his dissertation, *Husserl's Phenomenology of Perception: from Transcendental to Existential Phenomenology.*[6] Imagine an attractive member of the opposite sex walking in front some paces. Her light brown hair falls gently upon her shoulders and her walk shows a dance-like gait. She bouncingly continues to the end of the block where we make a discovery. She turns the corner and we are surprised: she is actually a boy. In one stoke everything has changed. Now the so-called sensations have become transformed. Her hair appears a bit stringier; it falls upon muscular shoulders; and her dance-like gait now looks more athletic. But sensations are supposed to be the stuff from which perception is built; it is not expected that the overall significance of the object affects sensory values. Here we come to another feature of the word-play which the French word *sens* offers. *Sens*, besides "sense" and "direction" may also mean "significance." Now we find that it is not the directedness of the perception to other parts of the field; but the fact that the significance of the perception, the meaning of the thing, shapes our reading of sensations. In passing we may note that Heidegger's overview of these two errors in the ontology of the thing is worth bearing in mind. He states: "Whereas the first interpretation [the substance/attribute ontology] keeps the thing at arms length from us, and sets it too far off, the second [the thing as a collection of sensations] makes it press too hard upon us."[7] The first tradition removes us from the world; the second hides it by bringing it too close.

Heidegger charts a third and last main tradition of the thing. This one also is rooted in Greek philosophy, particularly as expressed by the notions of *eidos* and *hyle*. This is the tradition which marks the development of notions of matter and form. We might note that Merleau-Ponty in *The Structure of Behavior* is somewhat in the grips of this ontology. Gestalt, after all, is a kind of form. However, as we have seen in the previous chapter, Merleau-Ponty "bursts", so to speak, the notion of Gestalt as form to include a structure where the whole always intimates a development which surpasses itself. In *The Phenomenology of Perception* the notion of a strictly delineated form is even more remote to his purposes. Heidegger's critique of this ontology turns primarily upon the fact that matter and form are themselves derivative of the uses or projects into which a thing is drawn. The hammer has a form: the shape one would see along side its name in a dictionary. The hammer's matter—the stuff it is made out of—is wood and iron. But hammers can be made out of aluminum or gold. Future hammers may have different shapes altogether—they may be computerized and look square. Both the form and matter could fully change without our saying we no longer have a hammer. Human projects and use determines the meaning of a thing, not matter or form. Nonetheless the matter/form ontology has powerful conceptual reign over great expanses of human practices and disciplines. Consider the force of this basic ontology on theories of logic and meaning, traditions of art and architecture and concepts of space and time.

The primary offense of this ontology for Merleau-Ponty arises by its denial of indeterminacy. If all things are formed matter, then the unformed does not count among things in the world. In Merleau-Ponty's view positive indeterminacy, that is the holding that something is there, although we are not clear what, is a feature of all objects and of all dimensions in the perceptual field. As he states:

> Although the landscape before my eyes may well herald the features of the one which is hidden behind the hill, it does so only subject to a certain degree of indeterminacy: here there are meadows, over there perhaps woods, and in any case, beyond near the horizon, I know that there will be land or sea, beyond that either open sea or frozen sea, beyond that either earth or sky and, as far as the limits of the earth's atmosphere are concerned, I know only that there is, in the most general terms, something to be perceived, and of those remote regions I possess only the style in the abstract. (Ph.P, p. 331; PP p. 382)

Indeterminacy, moreover, is not to be allocated only to exterior horizons. It is part of the foreground and the hidden sides of any object. As he claims, if perception were made only of distinctly formed objects:

> We ought then to perceive a segment of the world precisely delimited, surrounded by a zone of blackness, packed full of qualities with no intervals in between held to together by definite relationships. (Ph. P, 5; PP, p. 11)

And later in remarking upon the not presently perceived as indeterminate:

> . . . what is behind my back is not without some element of visual presence. (Ph. P, p. 6; PP, p. 12)

In short the matter/form ontology leads us to forget interior and exterior horizons of all sorts.

3. The distinction between the objective and the pre-objective worlds

The excursus into Heidegger's work on the errors of traditional ontologies opens Merleau-Ponty's claim that there is a *prèjugé du monde* to ontological problems in the Western philosophical tradition in general. In Merleau-Ponty's view, philosophers and scientists accounting for perception have methodically asked the wrong questions about perception due to a faulty conception of the perceptual world. Merleau-Ponty distinguishes between a "pre-objective" and an "objective" world and maintains that theorists on perception are uniformly on the wrong track by insisting that the perceptual world is the objective world. The so-called objective world is actually laden with confusions and in fact incorporates all of the erroneous ontologies which Heidegger has detected. Those theorists who assume that the perceptual world is the objective world, even in view of the inconsistencies in maintaining this ontology, tend to hold to a substance/attribute view of a thing, attempt recurrently to explain perception in terms of sensations, and methodically attempt to eliminate elements of perceptual experience which are given as indistinct or indeterminate. The following chart, CHART I, indicates the main differences between the pre-objective and the objective world.

CHART I

Objective World	*Pre-objective World*
1. It is made up of independent objects which are context-free.	1. Things in this world are dependent upon the context that they appear in.
2. Features or properties of objects are distinct and fully determined.	2. Each change in a part of the thing alters the significance of the whole.
3. The objective world is the sum of these objects.	3. Aspects of things as well as expanses of the pre-objective world as a whole are taken to be "there" yet indeterminate.

The distinction between the objective and the pre-objective world can be understood by considering an optical illusion which Merleau-Ponty refers to in *The Phenomenology of Perception*, the Müller-Lyer illusion. (Ph. P, p. 6)

When we look at the two figures in the Muller-Lyer illusion paying ordinary attention to them we see figures which have a character or "physiognomy," to use one of Merleau-Ponty's favorite expressions. The top figure has a significance; it appears compact or concentrated. The lower figure looks sprawling.

Now when we are asked in which figure is the middle line longer, we *see* the middle line in the top figure as shorter and the middle line in the bottom figure as longer. The character or physiognomy of the figures plays into our perception to the extent that we judge length according to it. (Recall that *sens* for Merleau-Ponty entails significance as well as directedness.) The surprise comes when we are asked to measure the two middle lines. We find out that they are the same length. The apparent inequality between the two lines is now taken to be "illusory."

In Merleau-Ponty's terms the optical illusion reveals the fact that ordinarily we perceive a pre-objective world. In the pre-objective world things are given as wholes where the significance of the whole affects our perception of various features of the whole. They are not a collection of context-free qualities nor are the things themselves free from interrelationships to the perceptual field that they appear in. It is an error which has riddled centuries of theories of perception to hold that the "cramped" or "sprawling" physiognomies are overlaid upon context-free sensory data. The Müller-Lyer "illusion" demonstrates as much. In the top figure, the middle line looks shorter because we see the figure as having a certain character. Our judgments and reflections are built upon such physiognomies.

When we take a straight edge and measure the middle lines we shift to the so-called "objective world." This shift demands an extraction from the context in which the figures appear. We compare the middle line to the line of the straight edge, removing it from its relationship to the rest of the figure. We are then surprised to *see* the two lines as equal. What has actually occurred is that we have a line which *in relation to the former physiognomie*s is context-free. But no such shift, from Merleau-Ponty's point of view is ever wholly context-free. In this case, we are brought to notions which are context-free in relation to this immediate diagram but not context-free from the world of angles, curves etc, that is, a language of spatial idealizations. In fact, it is context-free only by being removed from the significances expressed by these figures.

4. The criticism of the Empiricist and Rationalist approaches to Perception

The introduction to the *Phenomenology of Perception* is subtitled "Traditional Prejudices and the Return to Phenomena." Traditional prejudices, from Merleau-Ponty's point of view, are based upon the distortion of the pre-objective world in favor of the objective world. But the traditional prejudices, he claims, observe two typical paradigms which express with increasing refinement the dichotomies of a the subject/object distinction. Again in a way that overlaps Heidegger's thought, Merleau-Ponty sees, in the philosophy of perception, the development of a subject/object ontology. As he states in the introduction:

> We started off from a world in itself which acted upon our eyes so as to cause us to see it, and now we have a consciousness or thought about the world . . . We pass from absolute objectivity to absolute subjectivity . . . (PhP p. 39; PP p. 49)

For Heidegger it is the destiny of Western thought to arrive at this ontological error expressed by the subject/object dichotomy. Science, theology, aesthetics and philosophy have all succumbed to it.[8] For Merleau-Ponty, the situation is somewhat different. A version of subject/object relations can be maintained but it needs to be understood in its origins in the lived body. For Merleau-Ponty notions of subject and object are derived from a single body/world interrelationship. Historically the interrelationship between subject and object has been misunderstood and has been set askew in favor of an idealized view of varying sides of the dichotomy. The "rationalist" has developed the notion of the subject; the "empiricist" the object. Both presume the objective world which leads both sides to erect explanatory schema which compound errors. And both the rationalist and empiricist accounts are not, as Merleau-Ponty presents them, restricted to topics associated directly with perception. They amount to epistemological ills which are syndromes, as it were;

similar errors are discussed within the entire range of topics presented in *The Phenomenology of Perception*. Thus empiricist and rationalist approaches influence speculation on the nature of freedom and time as well as influence theories of hallucination and the body image. In the two charts which follow, I have first, in CHART II, summarized the typical approaches associated with the empiricist and rationalist, and second, in CHART III, have noted the main differences attributed to the empiricist and rationalist as they appear in ten main topics in *The Phenomenology of Perception*.

Before turning to those charts, I would like to note two features of Merleau-Ponty's distinction between the empiricist and the rationalist. First, although he includes specific philosophers under these headings—in particular Descartes and Kant among the rationalists—he refers most often to thematic conceptual constructions which enable him to speak along the lines of epistemological types. He refers in general for example to "empiricist philosophy," "empiricist constructions" and "empiricist doctrine." (Ph.P pp. 23–4; PP pp. 31–2) We are left to interpret his view as the designation of a conceptual tradition which influences thinkers to ask certain questions and to accept certain sorts of answers. Accordingly, the same conceptual "landscape" might direct a philosophy student toward rationalism, for example, inasmuch as he has adopted the lines of questioning of his instructors, even in view of the fact that he has never read Kant or Leibniz. It actually becomes suitable then to speak of epistemological types since it is not the specific theories which are influential but pervasive conceptual tendencies which are ubiquitous, appearing regularly in psychologists and physiologists without any direct familiarity with the main influences of these epistemological traditions.

I would also like to note that various historians of philosophy have also discovered the tendency to explain perception "passively" through the accretion of sensations or mentalistically through the work of a faculty of attention or judgment. D. W. Hamlyn, currently the editor of *Mind*, states in his *Sensation and Perception, a History of the Philosophy of Perception*:[9]

. . . there have been two main tendencies in giving an account of perception. The first is to assimilate it to something passive as sensation might be supposed to be. The second is to assimilate it to judgement.

Merleau-Ponty's approach differs from this historical approach by his placing of theae traditions in the context of pervasive ontological errors.

CHART II
SUMMARY OF EMPIRICIST AND RATIONALIST
APPROACHES TO PERCEPTION

	Empiricist	*Rationalist*
Perceiving Subject	'a record book'—a tallying of experiences	a central constituting ego
Perceptual Field	a conglomeration of perceptual units	the totality of syntheses made upon a pre-perceptual given
Starting Point of Each Tradition's Analysis	the context-free perceptual unit	mentalistic faculties that are needed to clarify perceptual experience
Subsequent Attitude Towards the Pre-Objective World	a disordering of the perceptual mechanism	confusion out of which objects are produced

Fundamental Error

Pre-objective world denied in favor of assuming the ontology of the objective world

CHART III

<table>
<tr><td>Philosophical Viewpoints
Associated with Empiricism</td><td>Philosophical Viewpoints
Associated with Rationalism</td></tr>
<tr><td colspan="2" align="center">Body Image</td></tr>
<tr><td>body image accounted for as the summation of independently operating stimulus receptors (cf. Ph.P p. 76; PP pp. 90-1)</td><td>body image is taken to be purely "psychic." It is thought to be an idea of belief. (cf. Ph.P p. 77; PP p 91-2)</td></tr>
<tr><td colspan="2" align="center">Verbal Meaning</td></tr>
<tr><td>language viewed as a depository of phonemes associated with verbal images (cf. Ph.P p. 176; PP pp. 204-5)</td><td>words are though to be signs for mental entities i. e. thoughts or ideas. (cf. Ph.P p. 177; PP pp. 205-6)</td></tr>
<tr><td colspan="2" align="center">Interworking of Senses</td></tr>
<tr><td>each sense is viewed as a receptor for categorially different kinds of data. (cf. Ph.P p. 218; PP pp. 251-3)</td><td>senses seen as different avenues through which the same world is distinguished (cf. Ph.P pp. 217-8; PP p. 251-3)</td></tr>
<tr><td colspan="2" align="center">Verticality</td></tr>
<tr><td>"up" and "down" assumed to exist in the world apart from the perceiver's orientation (cf. Ph.P p. 247; PP p. 286)</td><td>"up" and "down" seen as relationships dependent upon arbitrarily chosen fixed points. (cf. Ph.P p. 247; PP p. 286)</td></tr>
<tr><td colspan="2" align="center">Depth</td></tr>
<tr><td>height and breadth are perceived immediately but depth is sensed only through remembering what an object looks like from different sides. (cf. Ph.P p. 255ff; PP pp. 295ff)</td><td>depth understood through connecting an object with a concept of space. (cf. Ph.P pp. 255ff; PP pp. 295ff.)</td></tr>
</table>

Hallucinations

physiological explanations are construed so that "the irritation, for example, of certain nervous centers cause sense-data to appear as they appear in perception through the action of physical stimuli on those same nervous centers." (cf. Ph.P p. 335; PP pp. 386-7)	"a pure *cogitatum* of the *cogito* which it possesses and constitutes in its entirety." (cf. Ph.P pp. 336-7; PP pp. 387-9)

Cogito

a series of psychic events (cf. Ph.P p. 372; PP p. 426)	a central constituting subject or ego (cf. Ph.P p. 372; PP p. 425)

Temporality

successive instances of a "now" (cf. Ph.P p. 412; PP. p. 471-2)	a structure generated by an ego which is itself out of time. (cf. Ph.P p. 426; PP pp. 487-8)

Freedom

determinism; our behavior is the result of the interaction of mechanistically conceived parts (cf. Ph.P pp. 436-7; PP pp. 498-9)	unrestricted freedom in that the constituting ego is ultimately responsible for the way the world is organized. (cf. Ph.P pp. 436ff; PP pp. 499ff.)

The World

the collection of objects existing in the world. (cf. Ph.P p. 281; PP p. 325)	the law which governs veridical perceptions (cf. Ph.P p. 281; PP p. 325)

Let us consider the development marked in CHART II. The "fundamental error" is for both the empiricist and rationalist traditions a denial of the pre-objective world and the maintaining

56

of a prejudice in favor of the "objective" world. This means that context-free, fully determinate, perceptual units are presumed to be the elements of perception. I will review the main developments in the histories of the two traditions which have been schematized in the chart.

First let us consider the empiricist's position. Merleau-Ponty offers the following example: "If I walk along a shore towards a ship which has run aground, and the funnel or masts merge into the forest bordering on a sand dune, there will be a moment when these details suddenly become part of the ship, and indissolubly fused with it". (PhP. p. 17; PP p. 24) How can we assume the Gestalt switch wherein we discover the ship in the forest from the point of view of traditional empiricism. Simply stated, there are two main possibilities. Either the ship is taken to be a collection of units of sensation or—in a manner for which our imagination is hard-pressed to conceive—the ship is taken to be one large perceptual datum. If we hold to the first case, we need to explain how the perceptual data come to be seen as one ship. Traditionally theories of association are introduced. One sense-datum leads to another. Perception is conceived, as I have indicated on the chart, as a tallying or conglomerating of sensory data. A great variety of hypotheses may be offered to explain how the association of sense data proceeds. But this much may said for this approach in general. As long as we are discussing direct evidence for perception itself, we must say it does not match our experience. We need only return to elements of Gestalt psychology to account for why: the Gestalt switch, in this case the discovery of the ship, occurs at one stroke. We have no experience of collecting sense-data. Furthermore if the empiricist insists that a collecting of sense-data occurs on a physiological level we must question his dedication to the model involved. He is endeavoring to give a theoretical account which presumes a mechanistic model. (In the empiricist's schema sense-data are tabulated without an appeal to intentions or goals.) But, Merleau-Ponty has already shown in *The Structure of Behavior* that we have no reason to believe that the mechanistic model, which the association of sensations implies, is an adequate one.

As to the alternative, that the whole object, in this case the ship in the forest, might be one large sense-datum, we do meet our experience of discovering the object at one stroke. But how far can this notion be extended? Shall we also suppose that the background to the ship is also a broad and complex sense-datum? If we accept Merleau-Ponty's description of the perceptual field as containing indeterminate regions—a thesis which matches our perceptual experience—we are again at loggerheads with the empiricist's assumptions. Can we make sense of an indeterminate sense-datum? Does not the very notion of a sense-datum presume distinct qualities? This implies that the project of building perception out of sensations or sense-data does not adequately fit our perceptual life.

Traditionally there is a third move that the empiricist may make. He may admit that we do not experience *seriatim* patches of data. We have instead few key sensations which trigger off a "projection of memories." Here sense-data drawn from memory are added to the process of association. But problems encountered in the simpler version of empiricism are now still present; they are only removed by muddling the role of memory in perception. In fact the introduction of memory is unnecessary to this approach and may be removed by an application of Occam's razor.

> How could the evocation of memories come about unless guided by the look of strictly visible data, and if it is thus guided, what use is it then, since the word (or object) already has its features before taking anything from the storehouse of memory. (Ph.P p. 20; PP p. 28)

The empiricist in attempting to sustain the notion of perception as a collection of data comes to allow the importance of the significance or meaning of the perceptual object. But this removes him, even in this more sophisticated model, from the "objective" ontology he would support.

The main moves of the rationalist's account are not as contrary to the empiricist's as they would seem. Descartes, from Merleau-Ponty's point of view, begins with a position which is phenomenologically more accurate than the empiricist's. He initiates a tradition which accepts that lack of clarity is an issue in perception. He sees hats and cloaks from his window; he does not in immediate experience see passers-by. And the ball of wax, Descartes' example in the Second Meditation, he admits, has no fixed properties. Thus at the onset of his investigations Descartes admits undefined perceptual data. But the admission is finally not tolerated in view of the criteria he observes for physical objects. The true object, the one that possesses clear and distinct qualities, is perceived through the faculty of attention. The faculty of attention discovers qualities which were already there. In so saying Descartes promotes a tradition which makes objectivity the result of a mental faculty. And, the remarkable analyses that Kant brings to the philosophy of perception are still in keeping with this presumption: we do not have an object until a mental faculty has been applied to some manner of unformed, pre-perceptual stuff. Hence my account in CHART II of the starting point of the rationalist tradition.

The characteristic error of this tradition becomes clear if we inquire into the role of the pre-formed stuff upon which the mind applies its definitive concepts or syntheses. Consider the Kantian position. We do not have an object until the manifold of intuitions is brought under categories of the understanding which establish for us the existence of a substance. But Kant presumes here that objectivity is identified with the substance/attribute ontology. Once this move is made, anything which does not fit this concept of an object is not validated as a thing. But to whom should we appeal for the correctness of this ontology? If we return to our perceptual life, this ontological framework at best only applies in removal from our direct experience. Furthermore, the effects of assuming such an ontology are grave. Perceptual life, which is given as founded in things which are already significant apart from their objectification, is denigrated into some manner of pre-perception. And the relation of the perceptual field to the perceiver is set askew by making the perceiver increasingly into the creator of his world. By observing that there is a pre-formed aspect to perception, the rationalist moves increasingly towards the position of holding that the world is ultimately the product of a wholly unworldly subject. This is quite a price to pay for the substance/attribute ontology. It is paid, moreover, at the expense of denying the existence of a pre-objective world.

CHART III is fairly self-explanatory if the characterizations of the empiricist and rationalist positions are clear. Throughout *The Phenomenology of Perception* Merleau-Ponty prepares his own account of the issues listed by undoing the force of the empiricist and rationalist approaches. Sketches of the traditional accounts for these issues are itemized on the chart. I have encapsulized the traditional positions and refer the reader to primary occasions in the text where they are discussed.

5. A difficulty in establishing the intellectual influences of Merleau-Ponty's theory of the body-subject.

Behind thy thoughts and feelings, my brother, there is a mighty lord, an unknown sage—it is called Self; it dwelleth in thy body, it is thy body.
—Nietzsche, *Thus Spake Zarathustra*[10]

In the twentieth century, many thinkers besides Merleau-Ponty made the body into a central philosophical issue. This is particularly true among French philosophers. Gabriel Marcel, for example, at the end of his *Metaphysical Journal* concludes that "I am my body."[11] Bergson begins *Matter and Memory* with a discussion of the importance of the body image.[12] And Sartre devotes lengthy sections of Part III of *Being and Nothingness* to an analysis of the body as a fundamental modality of being-in-the-world.[13] Merleau-Ponty was aware of the work of these thinkers. But it is likely that there was an abiding conviction that the body was the subject of personal identity long before it was offered as a philosophical viewpoint. Foucault indicates how certain sets of social practices just take for granted that personal subjectivity is bodily subjectivity. (For Foucault the sensibilities of a culture are disclosed in social practices.) In *Discipline and Punish*, he records the ingenuity that went into forming different manners of personal identity through the establishment of practices that moulded bodily behavior. There is a clear institutionalizing of practices in France and England in the 18th and 19th centuries which developed the "docile body," particularly suitable for working in workshops, barracks, prisons and hospitals.[14] Some of the people who institutionalized the schedules and regulations in hospitals or prisons may have been Cartesians and believed their bodies were machines and that they were "thinking things." Nonetheless, when they set about trying to mould the behavior of large sections of the population they set themselves to establishing new controls and disciplines for the body. There is no proof here, of course, that personal identity is to be equated with the body. But it seems fair to say that reflecting upon such actions tends to put the burden of proof more upon the one who argues that personal identity can be attributed to a disembodied mind, spirit or soul.

The work of Foucault puts Merleau-Ponty's theory of the body-subject into a special light. Are we to see his work as a response to the work of his philosophical predecessors—what I have called in earlier "a personal intellectual narrative?" Obviously, in certain ways it is. But tracing philosophical ancestry is, as I have argued, deceptive. If Foucault is right and social practices indicate that the European civilization has in its social understanding presumed for centuries that we are primarily our bodies, proposing a theory of the body-subject becomes more the occasion for the breaking of illusions that might overlay a society than a moment in the self-contained progress of ideas. The quote I have cited above from Nietzsche, similarly, is written in a manner which suggests he would dispel illusions. Nietzsche suggests not an arrival at a stage in the philosophical dialectic, nor even less a consequence drawn from lasting philosophical truths. Nietzsche's statement indicates he is asserting what those who have not had to succumb to social myths have known all along.

Now then taking into account such considerations, if we set about to place Merleau-Ponty's theory of the body into an intellectual historical context alone, we need to point out that such an approach invites a somewhat narrow view of intellectual progress. We are likely dealing with a manner of social honesty which may have little to do with the progress of ideas. Perhaps the progress of ideas is just what is questioned. The ideas of high culture may become so overwhelmingly at odds with sensibilities revealed in social practices that a thinker may come along who, perhaps in outrage, simply begins to consider what has long been an issue but not discussed. This was likely Nietzsche's position, and in my opinion, by topic, although not by treatment or manner of presentation, Merleau-Ponty's.

We should note however that we invite confusions in suggesting that Merleau-Ponty exhibits social honesty by professing a *theory* of how we are our bodies. In our ordinary behavior we act as if we never doubt that we are our bodies, regardless of what one might say in a philosophy or psychology class. But this ground presumption becomes steeped with errors as soon as we attempt to explain how we are our bodies. We are perhaps led to think: We are our bodies; therefore we are machines. We are our bodies; therefore we are bio-computers. We are our bodies; therefore we are bio-chemical composites, etc. The insufficiency of these concepts of the body leads us to find the identity in error. We are quite easily tempted to believe that we must fall back upon a notion of the mind to compensate for what the body as machine has not provided. But in so saying, we have not really begun properly. We have not carefully examined the models which we assume for the body. Quite clearly, Nietzsche, in the quote above, speaking of the body as a "great Lord," is not referring to a mechanistically conceived body. What Nietzsche evokes, Merleau-Ponty discusses in great detail. For Merleau-Ponty, we are our bodies, but established models of how we are our bodies are in error. In daily activities, we presume we are our bodies until we shift to the theoretical attitude and find our theories to be inadequate. In a sense,

Merleau-Ponty's work on the body is primarily geared to expose the correctness of our practical intuition and to correct our manners of assuming a theoretical attitude.

Let us consider, then, Merleau-Ponty's view of the body. We shall first consider its main properties as seen in relationship to perceptual life. Later we will discuss how it is taken to be foundational for language and reflection.

6. What the body-subject is not

First, an explanation of terminology. As indicated, I will be using the term "body-subject" for Merleau-Ponty's notion of the body. In *The Phenomenology of Perception* several different phrases are used for the body. Frequently one finds the "body proper" (*corps propre*), but also the "phenomenal body" (*corps phénoménal*) and the "habitual body" (*corps habituel*). Each one of these terms emphasize one aspect of the body over another. Since in *The Phenomenology* the body always functions within a system and counts as a "subject-side" of a subject/world system, however, the expression, the "body-subject," counts as an appropriate general term for this fundamental notion.

Further distinctions must be drawn to avoid confusions. The body-subject is not a conventional concept of the body. Ordinarily, depending upon whether macroscopic or microscopic levels are given to our discussion of the body, we conceive of the body according to its systems i. e. neurological, skeletal, digestive, endocrinological, etc., wherein attributes or features are predicated of these systems. Considering the body on microscopic levels, we conceive of it histologically cellularly, biochemically, etc., again predicating attributes to the main notions of tissues, cells, enzymes, etc. This approach to the body observes the substance/attribute ontology. I will call the version of the body implied here, the *objective body*. From Merleau-Ponty's point of view this approach is problematic insofar as it leaves out the pre-objective manner in which the body is "in a pact" with the natural world. Merleau-Ponty's concept of the body-subject parallels Heidegger's concept of *Da-sein* insofar as it demands an ontological revision if it is to be properly conceived.

Although what I am calling the objective body indicates our most familiar approach to the body, there is a second main way of conceiving the body. It also needs to be distinguished from the body-subject. The body may be conceived of as an idea, a mental picture or representation. Feeling a pain in my side, I may conjure a picture or image I have of my body as I see the pain coming from my appendix. Here the body becomes the creation of the mind or intellect. I will refer to this version of the body as the *body as representation*. This intellectualist approach to the body, in spite of its apparent antithetical origins from the objective view, also obscures the way in which the body and the world stand in a reciprocal relation.

What then is Merleau-Ponty concept of the body-subject? An understanding of his view can be prepared through one of Merleau-Ponty's discussions which draws upon the history of painting. Merleau-Ponty throughout his career refers to the discoveries of painters. The notebooks of famous painters offer a wealth of material for a phenomenology of visual perception. In the case of Cezanne we have a record which marks the experience of developing a fresh manner of visual perception. Let us turn to that description.

7. The "pact" formed between the body-subject and the natural world

Cezanne's major concern was "to depict matter as it takes on form, the birth of order through spontaneous organization." (SNS p. 13) "It is Cezanne's genius that when the overall composition of the picture is seen globally, perspectival distortions are no longer visible in their own right but contribute, as they do in natural vision, to the impression of an emerging order, of an object in the act of appearing, organizing itself before our eyes." (SNS p. 17) In short, Cezanne's paintings capture the moment when ghosts of color, shape and texture come to be collected into a thing. If we look at Cezanne's painting, "Jas de Bouffan," for example, we see first shapes that do not fit together. The three-storied building on the left is awkwardly leaning on one side. The disharmonious sides of the smaller buildings on the right seem also unworldly. They contain walls that do not permit us to incorporate them into whole things. If one stays with the picture, however, and explores the various disconnected shapes, a moment occurs when we seem to see into the picture. The various misfitting shapes and colors congeal into a very worldly scene. Cezanne returns us to the experience wherein a thing comes into being.

Cezanne's preparation for painting is revealing. According to his biographer, Gasquet, Cezanne would "halt and look at everything with widened eyes," "germinating" with the countryside. (SNS p. 17) But then his germinating would reach its goal; he was then known to exclaim, "I have the motif." He explained this moment of arrival as a "joining of hands with nature." Cezanne, himself, describes this moment by saying, "the landscape thinks itself within me." (SNS p. 17) At that time, there was a union formed between Cezanne and the landscape. And, immediately after that point, he began to sketch the "geological skeleton" of the painting. Now we may take this moment at the end of Cezanne's germinating, as paradigmatic of the point at which the body-subject and the perceptual field come together. Out of this union a spectacle in organized from the formerly vague regions within the perceptual field.

The relationship that takes place between the body subject and the perceptual field is referred to variously as a "coupling" (s'accoupler) (Ph.P p. 214; PP p. 248), a "communion" (Ph.P p. 212, PP p. 246), a "synchrony" (Ph.P p. 211; PP p. 245), a "sympathetic relation" (Ph.P p. 214; PP p. 248) and a "co-existence" (Ph.P p. 214; PP p. 248). These various terms reflect Merleau-Ponty's view on the relation between the body-subject and the perceptual world or as he sometime states between the sentient and the sensible.

The sentient and the sensible do not stand in relation to each other as two mutually external terms, and sensation is not an invasion of the sentient by the sensible. It is my gaze which subtends color, and the movement of my hand which subtends the object's form, or rather my gaze pairs off with color and my hand with hardness or softness, and in this transaction between the subject of sensation and the sensible it cannot be held that one acts while the other suffers the action, or that one confers significance upon the other. (Ph.P p. 214; PP p. 247-8)

As suggested by Cezanne's statement "the landscape thinks itself in me" a main difficulty in understanding Merleau-Ponty's concept of the body-subject/natural world relation lies in verbalizing this relationship in a way that does not fix the nature of perceiving subject nor the object perceived prior to the reciprocal action that takes place between them. Cezanne's saying that "the landscape thinks itself in me," in expressing a blend between the self/world relation, signals this problem.

In Merleau-Ponty's view, the body-subject does not have *specific* intentions nor direction towards the world. There is a teleology of the body. The body is motivated to establish the constancy of the object. In doing so it reduces tensions that exist between it and the perceptual field. In short, Merleau-Ponty conceives perception as a manner of adjusting to an array of different disequilibria. We might note that the effect of the approach is to offer a reversal of traditional approaches to perception which would see perception as an activity performed upon "appearances." Structures may be isolated in relation to the perception of depth, size, shape and color constancy but they are motivated finally by an equilibrium which is achieved wherein a thing is perceived in maximal clarity and richness. It is a fundamental project of the body-subject to establish such an equilibrium. In effect then, Merleau-Ponty parts company from traditional theories of perception which would make a distinction between sensation and perception. The body/world system is in disequilibrium prior to perception; there is no half-way house prior to perception where a perceiver reflects upon sensations. If the distinction between sensation and perception can be maintained at all, its relation should be reversed. As he

66

often states, "perception goes straight to the thing." (Ph.P p. 305; PP p. 352). The appearance of things under various perspectives are abstractions from lived perception and are derived from a primary teleology of the perceiving subject which establishes the constancy of the thing. As he states at the opening of the chapter entitled "The Thing and the Natural World:"

A thing has in the first place *its* size and *its* shape throughout variations of perspective which are merely apparent. We do not attribute these appearances to the object itself. They are an accident of our relations with it; they do not concern the object itself. (Ph.P p. 299; PP p. 345)

The primacy of the constancy of the thing can be illustrated by considering Merleau-Ponty's approach to the perceptual constancies. (The constancies of shape, size, and color, among others are accounted for in detail in *The Phenomenology*). Merleau-Ponty's arguments are complex. But his approach can be understood through an outline of his arguments. In general, his work on perceptual constancies consists in showing that in all cases 1) the body attempts to establish a maximum articulation of the perceptual object; 2) the establishment of maximum articulation involves the establishing of "levels" or "norms" according to which other objects are given a relative significance; 3) an integration of levels or norms is maintained by the body-subject by virtue of its being involved in a situation.

Let us consider size constancy first. According to accounts of perception which would base perception on sensation, when we see a man at a distance our perception of size constancy arises by comparing the "apparent image" of the man with other sensory cues. By comparing the apparent size of the man with cues drawn from the convergence of the eyes, for example, we establish size constancy. This approach is typical in that it would formulate a perceptual constancy from appearances. But this approach obscures how the perception of the thing precedes the reflection upon appearances.

> . . . is not a man *smaller* at two hundred yards than at five yards away? He becomes so if I isolate him from the perceived context and measure his apparent size: he is anterior to equality and inequality; he is the *same man seen from farther away*. One can only say that the man two hundred yards away is a much less distinguishable figure, that he presents fewer and less identifiable points on which my eyes can fasten, that he is less strictly geared to my powers of exploration. (Ph.P. p. 261; PP p. 302)

The man seen in the distance is not the same sort of object as the man seen close. We do not compare miniature figures with distance and compute the constant size since the man in the distance does not offer sufficient detail to allow for such an equivalence. In general, objects in the distance do not offer a richness of detail for my gaze; they are blurred or vague. Objects which are too close do not allow us to perceive their shape; we perceive only some parts of their surface. The body-subject requires an optimum distance, a *maximum prise*, to see an object as one in a museum needs to position oneself at the right distance to see a canvass. But note, it is not a question of having an appearance which one measures according perceptual cues to establish size constancy. Instead one has a manner of reciprocity or "coupling", determined by the requirements of the body subject, which are brought to bear upon the sentient/sensible interrelation and which establishes the *maximum prise*. This level of optimal distance thereafter does become a standard by which size can further be established. But as a standard it is formed in the act of perception. It is not an intellectual rule or criterion which is administered to different perceptual fields. It is in a constant state of renewal as the body-subject establishes how it can maximally be at grips or have a hold upon a thing.

Let us consider color constancy. Merleau-Ponty's understanding of color constancy is exceedingly rich. As has often been noted by anthropologists, the perception of color is subject to broad cultural differences. "The Maoris have 3000 names of colors." (Ph.P p. 305; PP p. 352). The Greeks of the classical age did not distinguish, as do we, between blue and black. From Merleau-Ponty's point of view these facts do not lead to questions as to the refinements of the Maoris' color perception or the classical Greeks' lack of it. Rather they depend upon a more fundamental issue. The perception of color constancy depends upon the constancy of the object not *vice versa*. Although a child can distinguish differences in the black/white continuum from birth, color perception develops relatively late in children. It develops appreciably after the naming and recognition of an object. In Merleau-Ponty's view, the multitude of colors named by the Maori indicates the primacy of distinguishing things over colors. The 3000 colors names of the Maoris do not indicate more distinctions in hue and saturation but less abstraction from the things themselves. In other words, the case of the Maoris reflects upon their manner of abstraction from things and not upon color sensitivity taken objectively.

In Merleau-Ponty's view, questions involving the perception of color have often been misposed because philosophy and perceptual psychology have failed to take into account that color perception operates differently depending upon whether the color is of an object, an area, or of a transparent medium. "The differential thresholds are lower in the case of surface colors than in colored areas." (Ph.P p. 306; PP p. 353). ("Surface colors" refers to colors on clearly delineated objects; "colored areas" refers to color on unbounded locations, for example, the colors of an expanse of desert sand.) In a room which is painted one color, wherein one cannot easily delineate the boundaries of the color, the color is perceived with a "density" which is greater than the same color on an object. And as indicated above such "area colors" are distinguished according to different thresholds of saturation and hue. Now, for Merleau-Ponty, taking into account the different modes of colors, e. g. surface colors, or colors of whole areas, or glows of illumination, is crucial if we are to understand how color constancy is achieved.

The body, in establishing color constancy, operates similarly to the establishing of distance by "maximum prise." The questions put to the body are the same. How might a maximal richness and articulation be established within the visual field? What level is established by body-subject so as to allow for the maximum richness within the perceptual field? In the case of distance, a balance is struck where richness and clarity are in "inverse proportion" and reach a "certain point of maturity and a maximum." (Ph.P p. 318; PP p. 367) In the case of color perception, however, an atmospheric color is seized upon, "entered into" and established as a level. We must bear in mind that the prejudice in favor of the objective world hides the nature of colored areas and atmospheric colors. Our tendency is to want to assign each color to a clearly delineated object. This tendency appears early in our tradition. Consider Socrates' definition of figure in the *Meno*:[15] "Figure is the only thing which always follows color." Socrates' statement indicates that area and atmospheric colors are not being taken into account. What figure or shape "follows" the blue of the sky? In general, we may ask to what object should we attribute lighting, the most pervasive of atmospheric colors? Certainly not the source of lighting since lighting falls upon the whole visual field. As Merleau-Ponty points out, "the painter can represent the former [the color of lighting] by the distribution of light and shade on objects and omit the latter [the source of lighting] altogether. (Ph.P p. 306; PP p. 353) How then does the color of illumination appear for us? Merleau-Ponty's response is that as long as we have adjusted to a situation, the color of illumination is a "neutral." "Electric lighting, which appears yellow immediately upon leaving the daylight, soon ceases to have any definite color for us, and, if some remnant of daylight finds its way into the room, it is this "objectively neutral" light which seems to have a blue tint about it." (Ph.P p. 311; PP p. 359) Illumination does have a color if it intrudes upon a scene with another illumination. But when it is the source of coloration in the field it operates as a point-zero within the color spectrum. As in the case of distance, the perception of color depends upon our striking a level within the field as a whole. The atmospheric color, which is taken as the color of illumination, operates similarly to optimal distance. (Optimal distance for a cup on the table may be a few feet; for a mountain, several miles. Even so both are taken to be neither near nor far.) The optimal distance establishes a level from which near and far are understood. Similarly the color of illumination establishes a neutral level from which the other colors are established and discerned.

Again, as we have seen with size constancy, our capacity to make the color of illumination into a level does not imply that it is assumed as a standard from which the intellect infers the "true value" of colors. Instead the dominant color of the illumination becomes a "neutral" inasmuch as the body-subject roots itself through its tasks in a situation.[16] Merleau Ponty refers to Gelb's *Farbenkonstanz* for evidence to this point. It also may be observed in our everyday experience as we look out a window and find the daylight pale or a stark bluish-white. It does not help to reflect upon the spectacle to remove the bluish tinge from the spectacle. The lighting becomes neutral when we physically go outdoors and set about doing our business in the scene that before we had only seen as a vista. Merleau-Ponty refers to Gelb's careful noting of this experience:

> If in a brightly lit room, we observe a white disc placed in a shady corner, the constancy of the white is imperfect. It improves when we approach the shady zone containing the disc. It becomes perfect when we actually enter it. The shade does not become really a shade (and correspondingly the disc does not count as white) until it has ceased to be in front of us as something to be seen, but surrounds us, becoming our environment in which we establish ourselves. (Ph.P p. 311; PP p. 358–9)

And later in more general application.

> Taking up our abode in a certain setting of color, with the transposition which it entails, is a bodily operation, and I cannot effect it otherwise than by *entering into* the new atmosphere, because my body is my general power of inhabiting all the environments which the world contains, the key to all those transpositions and equivalences which keep it constant. (Ph P. p. 311; PP p. 359)

Color constancy, then, from Merleau-Ponty's point of view involves the main features we have found in size constancy. Again there is first an entering into the pact with the natural world. The body-subject interplays with the natural world and

71

directed by its teleology sets about to establish maximal clarity and richness. In the case of color perception, this implies that the full variation of the spectrum be located even if the objects are lit by red, yellow, or green light. By taking the color of illumination as a level, the variations in color differences can be perceived. "True colors" are colors that maintain the same difference in relation to each other. "Our perception in its entirety is animated by a logic which assigns to each object its determinate features in virtue of those of the rest . . ." (Ph.P p. 313; PP p. 361) When we enter a photographer's darkroom lit by a red light, for example, all objects appear reddish. As the red illumination becomes a level, the "true color values" are discerned. But this can also be understood by saying that the maximal differences between the colors of objects are perceived. Seeing all objects as reddish allows for minimal variety. Making the illumination into a neutral hue is tantamount to saying no monochromatic hue is given to each color by the lighting. Thus a maximization of color differences occurs. And as was the case in size constancy, taking illumination as a level arises not from an intellectual subject that is disinvolved and applies a rule or standard upon the spectacle. It occurs and is a product of the subject engaging in projects in some region of the natural world.

The third constancy we will discuss is shape constancy. Let us consider Merleau-Ponty's example of the perception of a face.

> To see a face is not to conceive the idea of a certain law of constitution to which the object invariably conforms throughout all its possible orientations, it is to take a certain hold upon it, to be able to follow on its surface a certain perceptual route with its ups and downs, and one just as unrecognizable taken in reverse . . . (Ph.P p. 253; PP p. 292)

The shape of on object is recognized, for Merleau-Ponty by the movement of the gaze or touch. An object is circular, for example, if the gaze does not impose a directional shift in the movement of the gaze. Merleau-Ponty is not suggesting here that the gaze or touch follows boundaries of an object. The gaze rather establishes a significant movement or direction which is enough to distinguish one object from another. Again the term *sens* with its multiple meanings of direction and significance is relevant. Shape constancy depends upon the ability to establish different directions of the gaze. Through the gaze we differentiate one structure from another candidate which might otherwise count as similar. As he notes in the ordinary experience of perceiving a face, "I may be familiar with a face without ever having perceived the color of the eyes in themselves." (Ph.P p. 11; PP p. 18) Recognizing a person entails the establishing of such a direction of the gaze. It is enough to follow certain characteristic lines of the eyebrows, nose, and smile to give us a recognition of a person. The caricaturist accomplishes this in a cartoon wherein through only a few thematic lines he conveys the identity of a political figure or film star.

The intellectualist who would explain shape constancy by a formula or rule which is applied in every instance of the object leaves out that we fail to recognize objects if they put us at odds with our spatial orientation. The perception of a face makes this point particularly evident. As long as the person I know is seen upright or even lying down I can still recognize the smile as the person's smile. If the person is reclining I could at least walk around the bed and see the person from the foot of the bed. I would then see the "normal" expression. But there is a limit to the capacity of the gaze to find a familiar expression. If the face is inverted, the sense of familiarity collapses. As Merleau-Ponty puts it: "Eyelashes and eyebrows assume an air of materiality such as I have never seen in them." (Ph.P p. 252; PP p. 292). The face takes on an utterly unnatural, even monstrous, aspect.

As we have seen with size and color constancy, the body-subject, in its efforts to maximize its grasp of the world, establishes levels. This also occurs in shape constancy. To be able to catch onto the characteristic look of a person, I need to be able to orient myself in relation to a typical manner of beginning and ending for my "visual gesture." A sense of the "top" and "bottom" of an object allows me to apply my gaze to the object, orienting how it lights upon the object. For Merleau-

Ponty, a sense of "top" and "bottom" again arises from establishing a level which maximizes the degree of articulation of the perceptual field.

The establishing of verticality particularly demonstrates the manner in which the body-subject reestablishes its "pact" with the natural world. Experiments involving glasses which invert the perceptual field demonstrate that the subject on the first day of wearing the glasses experiences a landscape which appears unreal and upside down. On the second day normal perception begins to reassert itself but the subject has the feeling that his body is upside down. From the third to the seventh day the subject progressively finds that the perceptual field takes on a normal position. But the readjustment is made "in proportion as the subject is *more active*." (Ph.P p. 244–5; PP p. 282–4)

How can we account for the way that our sense of "top" and "bottom" come to be re-established? The empiricist offers the following explanation: Up and down in the perceptual field are the result of associating perceptual data with points on our body that mark up and down, e. g. the head and feet. The floor is down because I see and associate it with my feet; the ceiling is up because it is associated with what I see of my head—because something hanging from the ceiling will first brush my head and face, etc. But this model of explanation is not successful. It does not explain why the subject, on the second day of the experiment, feels himself to be upside down, even though the perceptual field looks upright. According to the association model, this temporary reversal should not occur.

For the rationalist "up" and "down" occur through the constituting mind's positing an axis of coordinates. The constituting mind in this case is like a geometer and stipulates: let this be up and let this be down. Now, this account has no problem in handling how the field can look upright and the body upside down. The mind has simply been remiss in changing the up-down axis as it applied to the body. But although the rationalist can answer some questions which the empiricist cannot, what the rationalist still cannot explain is why the perceptual field looks inverted at all. For at least the first day, the subject senses that the perceptual field is upside down. But if these directions are simply stipulative, he should have no sense that something has gone topsy-turvy.

Neither the empiricist nor the rationalist position adequately explains that a readjustment of top-bottom orientation takes place more quickly *as the subject sets about accomplishing his daily tasks*. The shifts occurs neither by a point by point readjustment of objects to bodily positions (the empiricist's expectation), nor by a single conceptual reconstitution of the field (the rationalist's expectation). The reorientation takes place as the subject roots himself through bodily actions in a situation. It is enough to establish again actions such as walking, opening a cupboard or sitting down to correct the perceptual field. In other words the re-establishment of verticality follows upon the successful restitution of the relation between bodily projects and the responses received from the world. Once this relation is established the notion of a spatial level follows. It becomes a perceptual ground or basis in which the body can co-exist and allows for an optimization of vertical orientation in relation to tasks and actions.

> It [the spatial level] comes to rest when, between my body as the potentiality for certain movements, as the demand for certain preferential planes, and the spectacle perceived as an invitation to the same movements and the scene of the same actions, a pact is concluded which gives me the enjoyment of space and give to things direct power over my body. (Ph.P p. 250; PP p. 289).

In Merleau-Ponty's view then, we have in the case of shape constancy a "reading" of the object through the gaze. This reading may be accomplished at various angles but loses its significance if an object is turned in such a way that the overall level for directing the gaze—the level by which we establish verticality—no longer counts as a manner of organizing a field for maximal recognition. In the case of seeing a square, a tension arises as we approach turning it 90 degrees. As we near the quarter turn, our gaze takes another part of the figure to be "top" and, in one stroke, we see it as a diamond. If our perception operated by formulae which expressed the internal relations of the object, we would see the same figure, not first a square, then a diamond. This is what the intellectualist account would suppose. But because our gaze establishes a level to maximize the significance of its direction, two different objects are seen. And note, in both cases it is not a question of an apparent shape which is read as a regular quadrangle and subsequently interpreted as a square or a diamond. Rather, the directionality of the gaze prepares for perception without confronting a sensation or an appearance as an intermediary.

What may we conclude about the pact of the body-subject and natural world from this discussion of perceptual constancies? Of color constancy Merleau-Ponty states, "The constancy of color is only an abstract component of the constancy of things, which in turn is grounded in the primordial constancy of the world as the horizon of all our experiences." (Ph.P p. 313; PP p. 362). The same remark may be asserted about the other constancies. Apart from speaking the language of sensations or appearances out of which an object is discerned, one has what he refers to as a "transitional synthesis" (Ph.P pp. 30, 419; PP pp. 39, 480) between the body and the natural world. The perception of the object is fixed as the body-subject plunges into the field so as to once again establish levels and maximize the richness and clarity of the object. This union with the natural world is recommenced repeatedly. The object perceived is the result of a "transition" which would repeatedly readjust levels and the relation of an object to them. Or in other words, the perception of each object involves a transitional adjustment in the body-subject/natural world system. Thus, in each perception we return to the primary pact between the body and the world. Merleau-Ponty describes the relation of the body-subject to the natural world as one of "primal acquisition." (Ph.P p. 216; PP p. 250) This notion is an important one in Merleau-Ponty's thought: the body-subject stands in primal acquisition to the pact with the natural world. Its centrality should be stressed because it reflects Merleau-Ponty's unique position among existential thinkers. Merleau-

Ponty claims to offer a solution to the "dilemma of the *for-itself* and the *in-itself*." (Ph.P p. 215; PP p. 249) In using the terms for-itself and in-itself he alludes directly to Sartre's *Being and Nothingness*. But he is also referring to any ontology or metaphysics which would isolate a subject from an object. Through his notion of primal acquisition we are given his position on how we as human beings are "in-the-world." Unlike Heidegger, he describes a rootedness or involvement which precedes social and cultural practices. In Heidegger's view, human beings always disclose some manner of "throwness" (*Geworfenheit*). That is to say, we, as individuals, emerge from the social practices in which we have been cast. In Merleau-Ponty's view on the other hand we acquire a series of involvements including, among others, an involvement in the social world and history. As we shall see in a later chapter, these different fields of involvement are reciprocally founded upon each other. But let us note now that unlike Heidegger, Merleau-Ponty recognizes a primal manner of involvement that we re-encounter in each act of perception wherein we plunge into the world. He describes the way in which this primal involvement plays into our ordinary activities as follows:

> But the fact remains that the thing presents itself to the person who perceives it as a thing in itself, and poses the problem of a genuine *in-itself-for-us*. Ordinarily we do not notice this because our perception, in the context of everyday concerns, alights on things sufficiently attentively to discover in them their familiar presence, but not sufficiently to disclose the non-human element which lies hidden in them. But the thing holds itself aloof from us and remains self-sufficient. This will become clear if we suspend our ordinary preoccupations and pay a metaphysical and disinterested attention to it. It is then hostile and alien, no longer an interlocutor, but a resolutely silent Other, a Self which evades us no less than does intimacy with an outside consciousness. (Ph.P p. 322; PP p. 372)

The "in-itself-for-us" he speaks of above is a means of responding to the for-itself/in-itself dilemma. Given the pact between the body and the world the Sartrian dichotomy collapses. The "in-itself-for-us" is the fundamental merging out of which the integrity of subject and object come to be forged. The "resolutely silent Other" refers to the natural world, "resolute and silent" only in relation to its difference from our familiar social world with its tools and manners that accomodate themselves to a quick reading of their significance.

8. The anonymity of the body-subject: the pre-personal one

In Merleau-Ponty's view, the body-subject is not a personal subject in the sense that the self who makes decisions, choices and reflections is. Merleau-Ponty refers to the identity of the body-subject as "pre-personal" (Ph.P. pp. 84, 208, 216, 240, 352; *PP* pp. 99, 241, 250, 277, 405). The body, "plays beneath" (Ph.P. p. 84; PP p. 99) our personal existence. Occasionally we experience the subjectivity of our own body. It is then sensed as an "anonymous one" (Ph.P. p. 240; PP p. 277).

The subjectivity of the body normally continues unnoticed. As long as personal decisions, reflections, choices, etc., are not in disagreement with body-projects, we overlook the body-subject. We take it for granted, for example, that the body will bring an unclear spectacle into focus. If we direct our attention, however, to those times when personal decisions and planning conflict with ways the body is set to perform, we may witness the body's directedness. Merleau-Ponty discusses forms of behavioral disorders, i.e. cases of phantom limbs and anosognosia (Ph.P. pp. 80–89; PP pp. 90–105) which indicate the pre-personal aspect of the body-subject. Such disorders are relevant to an elucidation of a pre-personal body because individuals who suffer from such ailments seem to have one understanding—they recognize, for example, that a limb has been amputated—whereas their bodily behavior indicates that they maintain the projects associated with that limb. In Merleau-Ponty's view, such subjects continue to maintain and even feel sensations in the phantom limb as long as they "remain open to all the action of which [it] is alone capable; it is to retain the practical field which one enjoyed before the mutilation." (Ph.P p. 81–2; PP p. 97) In other words, the body in its involvement with the world maintains its own projects apart from an intellectual decision to change them. Correspondingly, the development of bodily projects may occur long before a conscious choice to do so.

Merleau-Ponty's sense of the body-subject as a pre-personal anonymous "one" can be witnessed on more ordinary occasions. Suppose that someone who enjoys French cuisine, for example, passes by a four star French restaurant which is famous for its beef bourguignon. He cannot resist it. He takes his seat and orders the dish, however, the waiter returns to say that the cook says it is not available. At such a moment, we expect our subject will be at odds with his intentions. It is almost as if the palate must be undone and reorganized before he can consider another dish. There is a split between personal and bodily "decisions." The man changes his plans. Even so, the change in plans is not total; he is still somewhat frustrated because the way his body has become set cannot be so easily undone. In this case the man may catch, out of the corner of his eye so to speak, a sense of the identity of the body in its readiness to eat the beef. The subject who still is ready to eat the beef is, strictly speaking, not his personal self. Yet he cannot will that it forget its intentions and preferences. But the body-subject directed toward a this meal is also not a mere, impersonal thing. It is a way that his own body has become prepared for a kind of activity. Indeed if one describes the readiness of my body at this point, it is neither an "I," a "You" nor even an "it" but a nameless, albeit directed, subject.

Merleau-Ponty's description of the body-subject as a pre-personal "one" has direct application to his theory of perception. Since it is the body we see with and the body is pre-personal, the objects we see are not taken to be products of your or my perception, but objects for perception in general. When someone learns how to type or ski, the typewriter and the skis are the correlates of the body's capacities. Granted one may claim personal ownership of such objects but such claims involve further refinements within the social world. The identity of the body-subject "plays beneath" such personal claims.

Consequently the objects, the typewriter or the skis, in their availability are also pre-personal. They are given as open to "anyone" who knows how to use them.

9. The directionality of the body-subject and the unity of the natural world

So far we have considered two main aspects of the body-subject: First, Merleau-Ponty's account of our rootedness or our manner of being-in-the-world, through the pact between the perceiving subject and object. Second, we discussed briefly the anonymity of the body-subject—how it is a pre-personal one. The last feature of the body-subject we will discuss is the "directionality" of the body-subject. The objects that we see are given as touchable and having scents, aromas and tastes even though we are not in reach of them. We live in a world where objects contain hidden sides and interiors and where the perceptual field extends indefinitely beyond our field of activity. For Merleau-Ponty these fundamental aspects of the natural world, the intersensoriality of the object and the maintenance of interior and exterior horizons[18] require an investigation of the body as a unity of "directionality" towards to the world.

We can understand the directionality of the body by considering the body's capacity to transpose skills. Any situated body-subject has a repertory of skills which it *can* do.[19] The capacity to retain and perform skills need not involve intellectual awareness nor the retention of a thinking subject. We learned how to walk, for example, in our infancy and the learning process itself has long since been forgotten. We easily overlook that a remarkable balancing act is involved. In spite of the fact that this skill was learned long ago, we are not aware of the specific moves made in walking. Do we choose to throw the weight of the body to the heel or to the ball of the foot? Clearly posing such questions to our reflecting consciousness is not relevant to our knowing how to walk.

We are hard pressed to explain body skills mechanically. The body, in performing a skill, manages to adjust itself to situations for which it may have had no previous experience. When we try to concoct a purely mechanical account, e. g. pressing weight on the heel causes, by reflex, the ball of the foot to press downward, which in turn pushes up and catches the weight of the body, etc., we fail to explain how, once we learn a skill, we can recreate that skill in circumstances that would call for systematically different mechanical explanations. Once we know how to walk, we can walk in shoes or barefoot, up steep walkways or down hills, even though, causally speaking, the types of muscular tension, parts of the feet, and degrees of body weight are greatly altered. Similarly, knowing how to sign one's name on paper opens the possibility of signing it on a blackboard or on sand, although the extension of limbs and positions of hands are point for point different.

In Merleau-Ponty's view the capacity of the body to reenact a skill under a variety of situations remains a confusion as long as one tries to conceive of the body as the "objective body." Beginning with this conception of the body, we are led to speculate how the various parts are coordinated within a task and how the coordination can be reformed as one walks for example in boots, or in sand. The prejudice in favor of the objective world has made a paradox out of the manner in which the body is directed to an object. Actually the parts of the body as described in an anatomy book only confuse the manner in which they are given significance as we perform a task. The body-subject in attempting to realize a goal gives a *functional* significance to parts of the body. Objective distinctions are both conceptually and practically irrelevant. In the case of walking, functional values which count as a capacity to propel the body and a capacity to cushion and further propel the body are allocated to parts of the body. But it is not the objective body to which these capacities are allocated. This again returns to the prejudice in favor of the objective world. Rather, it is the capacities themselves and their interrelationship which are primary. If there is a division that could be made in terms of bodily parts at all, it would involve establishing unusual identities between parts. As far as walking is concerned, the toe, the ball of the foot, or even the hand entail an effective identity since these parts could all serve to initiate a first step. They, in turn, have a functional relation to another set of body parts which count as capable of cushioning the movement of the first step. Walking in short defines the body and maintains a significance for the body, not the reverse. As Merleau-Ponty states:

> If I am sitting at my table and I want to reach the telephone, the movement of my hand towards it, the straightening of the upper part of my body, the tautening of the leg muscles are superimposed upon each other. I desire a certain result and the relevant tasks are spontaneously distributed among the appropriate segments, the possible combinations being presented in advance as equivalent . . . That is why, in their first attempts at grasping, children look, not at their hand, but at the object: the various parts of the body are known to us through their functional value only, and their coordination is not learnt. (Ph.P p. 149; PP p. 174)

Now if we add to the body-subject as defined by functional values the fact that these functional values are, in principle, polarized in the world, we have the backbone of Merleau-Ponty's account of intersensoriality of an object as well as interior and exterior horizons. Explanation is in order. Let us look specifically at the directionality of the body-subject in the areas of external horizons, internal horizons, and unity of the perceptual object.

Consider an example. The moon on the horizon appears huge, much larger than the moon overhead. If the moon is seen through a tube that isolates it from its background, however, it looks the same size regardless of its position in the field. As soon as the tubing is removed it appears again huge on the horizon. In Merleau-Ponty's view the phenomenon may be explained through the directionality of the body. The body is functionally related to the horizontal field differently than it is to the vertical field. Our bodily directionality extends outwards, not upwards. Few of our activities involve an ascent or descent that we can accomplish with our bodies. We are largely incapable of vertical movement except through mechanical means. (Apes, Koffka claimed, have "a vertical constancy which is faultless." Tree dwellers, because they can move freely up and down, have a body directionality which is global. Ph.P p. 304n; PP p. 350) For us, the horizontal dimension has more meaning than the vertical. The moon on the horizon appears larger, because the more greatly articulated horizontal field *means* for the body that the moon is at the end of a much greater expanse as understood by reference to bodily skills. (A similar experience occurs in time when a clustering of many important events leads us to feel that time is passing slowly.) The few skills we pursue overhead *mean* for the body that the vertical field is less expansive. So such a distance, having less significance, leads us to think the moon is smaller—it would have to be so if so little expanse separates us from it. The construction of space as organized by the body-subject, our "lived space," is rather like the often reprinted map of the United States which appeared on the cover of *The New Yorker* and which recapitulates the point of view of someone who makes New York City into the center of his universe. Ninth and Tenth Avenue in Manhattan are prominent and relatively large. New Jersey across the Hudson is somewhat smaller. Chicago is roughly in place although prominent for the most part just as a name. Nebraska, Kansas City, Las Vegas, and Los Angeles are the only places indicated as we proceed west and the national borders, properly indeterminate, are marked by inexact broken lines. This cartoon fits the mapping brought about through the polarization of the body-subject.

The case of the moon on the horizon is revealing of how the projects of the body shape our lived space. But it is important to see that the objects the body is polarized towards are unified in a way that matches the unity of the body. We move towards an object. We reset the functional values of the body as a whole since the plans or projects with the object are enacted by the body as a whole. The object is the recipient of the body's projects and reveals the body's unity.

A certain tactile experience felt in the upper arm signifies a certain tactile experience in the forearm and shoulder, along with a certain visual aspect of the same arm, not because the various tactile experiences among themselves, or the tactile and visual ones, are all involved in one intelligible arm, as the different facets of the cube are related to the idea of the cube, but because the arm seen and the arm touched, like different segments of the arm, together *perform* one and the same action. (Ph.P p. 151; PP p. 177)

Because the parts of the body are functionally interrelated, seeing a cup, for example, has meaning for various parts of the body besides the gaze. The visual aspects of the cup merge with the tactile and gustatory aspects. The intersensorial unity of the cup matches the unity of senses in the body. Let us consider further how this polarization of a communion of the senses is brought about.

The discussion of weight constancy in the chapter "The Thing and the Natural World" illustrates how the body unifies an object intersensorially. (Ph.P. p. 313; PP p. 362). An individual can identify the same object merely by its weight, regardless if he picks up the weight with his eyes closed, carries extra weight in his hand, lifts the object with his foot, teeth or forehead, or feels the weight in water. How can we account for the capacity of an ordinary individual to identify the same weight, even though he experiences it in such diverse ways? Can we say he identifies the weight through an intellectual understanding of how the same weight would affect his hand or foot or forehead? Even if the subject were extraordinarily adept at computing how the same weight would affect the hand in water versus the hand in air, for example, we could not explain the fact that the subject picks out the same weight by the "feel" of it alone. Shall we say, then, that the subject mechanically has built up ties of association with various weighing experiences, so that he knows that a certain pressure on the hand may be equated with a certain pressure on the foot? This explanation also is not satisfactory, since it is extremely unlikely that the individual has had the opportunity to make all the equations of association necessary. For example, it is extremely unlikely that he has had the occasion to feel this weight on his forehead or feel the weight under water.

Our capacity to perceive weight constancy is explained through what Merleau-Ponty calls a *schema corporel*. It is often described as a "system of equivalents and allows for sensorial and motor transpositions within the body. (Ph. P. p. 141; PP p. 165). But the term *schema corporel* translated problematically as "the body-image" easily confuses the sense of Merleau-Ponty's notion. The expression, bodily "schema," as well as "bodily image" suggests a network of relations in the body wherein some set kinaesthetic or sensorial data can be translated into another. But again we are led to think of fixed bits of data organized by an overriding schema or rule. Occasionally Merleau-Ponty suggests such a reading in saying, for example, "What we have called the body image is precisely this system of equivalents, the immediately given invariant whereby the different motor tasks are instantaneously transferable." (Ph.P. p. 141; PP p. 165). The term "invariant" here suggests a fixed network in the body which translates one sensation into another. But this is clearly not his intention. Statements such as the *schéma corporel* "is a system which is open to the world and correlative to it" more directly express his view. (Ph.P p. 143n; PP p. 168n) His saying that the *schéma corporel* "is open to the world" needs to be given its full weight. The openness he speaks of here is elemental to the *schéma corporel* since each aspect of the system of equivalences is from the beginning a directedness towards the world. The body-subject is organized by elements which have functional value, not by sensory data. When, for example, we feel a book in one hand and know how it would feel on the foot, we can do so because the hand is first given as a means towards certain actions, many of which implicate other parts of the body. The system of equivalents is analogous to a musical melody and not an equation. Like a melody each note is sensible in relation to the overall "gestural direction" of the melody. When, for example, we feel the texture of silk or wool and are thereby able to know what silk or wool would feel like on the back or stomach, even if we have never felt wool or silk on the back or the stomach before, we are engaged in an adjustment of sensory investigation which has already implicated these other parts of our body and allows us to adjust how the back would touch the silk in terms of how the hand has touched the silk. The key issue here is that in all cases the unity of the system of equivalences is a unity of directedness towards the world and not a unification of data.

We are now in a position to account for the intersensoriality of the thing and interior and exterior horizons. Just because the body through its actions unifies actions which are given as directed towards the world, our perception of an object as well as its background reflects the organization of the body-subject. It is not a question of mirroring or projecting. The thing and the world are the polarization of the body's directionality, while at the same time the constancy of objects and the world ensure and preserve the unity of the body. When I look at the cup of coffee on the table it is given as having weight, taste, smell, etc. It is enough for my gaze to be directed to the cup of coffee for its intersensorial aspects to be present for me, provided *my body as a whole is alerted to some actions in regards to the cup*. This can be tested in a simple experience. If I am actually seeing the cup, i. e. find in the cup an assurance of smell, taste and weight, etc., I notice that the noises outside my window are not yet the noise of things. In fact, they become the noise of something only when I stop looking at the cup and direct some action towards the noise. Then I hear the sound *of a car*, which at the same moment, I place in space. Conversely if I look at the cup of coffee, while at the same time maintaining the intention or project to move the table or close a door, the cup loses its ''presence''. It also loses its intersensoriality. It becomes a ''pre-thing'' having a vague visual aspect. There is no need to imagine that a mentalistic faculty of attention has unified these objects and positioned them in space. Listening to the car, amounts to establishing a directedness of my body towards the car. The directedness of the body as a whole alerts the sensory elements of the body in general. My hearing the car, for example, is not without an awareness of the smell of exhaust gases although the car is distant and I do not yet actually smell them. All that is required for the intersensoriality of an object is a directedness towards that object and a readiness to perform an action on the object. This directionality cannot be shared by objects to which we extend different tasks. Hence either the cup or car is given as present; not both at once.

The intersensoriality of the object, then, is a product of body teleology as it directs itself to an object. Merleau-Ponty understandably calls this manner of unity not a synthesis but a "synergy" since it is not a question of combining sensory elements but of aligning the body's action towards the object.

> It is not the epistemological subject who brings about the synthesis but the body, when it escapes from dispersion, pulls itself together and tends by all the means in its power towards one single goal of its own activity, and when one single intention is formed in it through the phenomenon of synergy (Ph.P. p. 232; PP p. 269).

Thus due to the synergy of the body . . . the brittleness, hardness, transparency and crystal ring of a glass all translate a single manner of being." (Ph.P p. 319; PP p. 368). This is because "the sensory 'properties' of the thing together constitute one and the same thing, just as my touch and all my other senses are together the powers of one and the same body integrated into one and the same action." (Ph.P p. 317–8; PP p. 367). And we add that the synergy of the body is not only a sufficient but also a necessary condition for the perception of a thing. Cases which fall short of this are "phantoms" or "pre-things." As he states: "If a phenomenon—for example, a reflection or a light gust of wind— strikes only one of my senses, it is a mere phantom, and it will come near to real existence only if, by some chance, it becomes capable of speaking to my other senses, as does the wind when, for example, it blows strongly and can be seen in the tumult it causes in the surrounding countryside," (Ph.P p. 318; PP p. 368)

External and internal horizons also can be explained through the directionality of the body-subject. Here Merleau-Ponty revises the conventional understanding of external and internal horizons which would conceive the horizons as fields of possibility. For Merleau-Ponty, both external and internal horizons are *present*, as much as objects are present.

> Through my perceptual field, with its spatial horizons, I am present to my surroundings, I co-exist with all the other landscapes which stretch out beyond it, and all these perspectives together form a single temporal wave, one of the world's instants. (Ph.P p. 331; PP p. 381)

In speaking of a "single temporal wave" Merleau-Ponty refers to his own corrections of existential theories of temporality. We shall discuss his view of temporality in a subsequent section (*vide* Chapt. 3, Sect. 5). What is most important for us to note now is that for Merleau-Ponty the spatial horizons are co-present with objects. They are treated as if they are a different kind of being, an indeterminate and general being, nonetheless a co-present kind of being. They complete the dimensions of our overall "field of presence." We need to return to the pact with the world which is our primal acquisition to discover the role that the spatial horizons play in Merleau-Ponty's account. As the body endeavors to establish *maximum prise*, internal and external horizons count as the "near" and "far" indeterminate regions which are balanced in bringing an object to maximal clarity. If the object is distant we are particularly open to exterior horizons. (A gaze has moved outward from the optimum distance.) If the object is closer than optimum we are particularly open in interior horizons. But in both cases, for Merleau-Ponty, they are not articulated fields which do not happen to be focused upon. (This view again presumes the priority of the objective world.) They are rather fundamentally indeterminate. External horizons may solicit or invite our attention in characteristic ways, as for example the horizontal field invites actions of greater complexity than the vertical field as we have seen with the moon on the horizon. But the actions solicited are not fixed and specifically prompted in advance. There is a genuine and positive indeterminacy to the perceptual horizons for Merleau-Ponty. In describing the perceptual horizons Merleau-Ponty is actually insisting on our recognizing a manner of being which is not a case of indeterminacy-which-is-actually-determinate when one observes the phenomenon, but an irrevocable indeterminacy which can only motivate general actions from the body-subject. The spatial horizons offer no property which is fixed or clear. They are regions in which the "questioning and answering" of the body-subject and natural world may take place. But they disappear or become background once an object becomes fixed. From this it is inconsistent to hold that the horizons are a collection of unclear *objects*, since the perceptual horizons always provide more possibilities than any collection of objects. Conversely objects always provide more clarity and exactitude than the spatial horizons.

How does Merleau-Ponty's theory of the body-subject account for the perceptual horizons? Just because the body-subject's intentions, as it plunges into the perceptual field, are general, the perceptual horizons as polarizations of this manner of directedness are general. Interior and exterior horizons are regions which are available to us in proportion to an object's proximity to us. When an object becomes "fixed" a specific directedness of the body is established. But this is a solution to a problem which the body-subject first faces neither with specific intentions; nor is it met with horizons which supply specific features from which the body-subject may choose.

10. Does Merleau-Ponty have a theory of authenticity in *The Phenomenology of Perception*?

. . . I knew, and it was an illumination—one of those things one has always known, but never really understood before—that all sanity depends on this: that it should be a delight to feel the roughness of a carpet under smooth soles, a delight to feel heat strike the skin, a delight to stand upright, knowing the bones are moving easily under the flesh. If this goes, then the conviction of life goes too.

—Doris Lessing, *The Golden Notebook*[17]

At the end of Section 7, on the pact between the body-subject and the natural world, I pointed out that Merleau-Ponty offers a unique manner of "being-in-the-world." Unlike Heidegger's view, where being-in-the-world is inextricably cultural, Merleau-Ponty's view depends on our emerging from a "primal acquisition." This primal acquisition is a background which is never wholly integrated into social and cultural involvements. The role of the body-subject, particularly in view of this "primal acquisition," alters the question of authenticity.

For both Heidegger and Sartre, authenticity (or good faith) reflect an either/or dichotomy. The notion of affirmation and denial, or at least acceptance and avoidance, are taken to reflect the fact that the basic positions one may take upon one's own existence are twofold. One may affirm one's choices and commitment or not. Merleau-Ponty's view differs on this issue.

In a case study discussed in the chapter entitled "The Body and its Sexual Being" Merleau-Ponty mentions the strained relevance of speaking of "bad-faith". A "girl whose mother has forbidden her to see again the young man with whom she is in love, cannot sleep, loses her appetite and finally her use of speech." (Ph.P p. 160; PP p. 187) Merleau-Ponty rejects a classical Freudian explanation which would explain the loss of speech in terms of an oral fixation which governs her present situation. His existential analysis stresses that the girl's dilemma is wholly played out in her body and is given its significance by the complexity of body-projects connected with the mouth. An oral psychosexual fixation is one dimension. But, speech and eating are also in question. Speech after all is a project which is "intimately linked with communal existence." (Ph.P p. 160; PP p. 187). The girl in losing her power of speech breaks the relational life within the family circle. From this case it seems possible to speak of a manner of bad faith or inauthenticity since the girl cannot accept her own involvement. But it would be more to the point to speak of a shrinking or contraction of the world which circumscribes what choices are available. The girl is not choosing not to speak; that part of the world is not available to her. For Merleau-Ponty it is not a question of a "stand" taken on one's existence. If authenticity is to have relevance at all, it involves a retreat or expansion—a redrawing of what will count as one's world. Once the boundaries are drawn, or withdrawn, choice and resolve, at least perceived from an intellectual decision-making point of view, are not at issue.

In a striking description. Merleau-Ponty points out how the experience of falling asleep offers a paradigm of how the body shuts itself off from the world.

> Loss of voice as a situation may be compared to sleep: I lie down in bed, on my left side, with my knees drawn up; I close my eyes and breathe slowly, putting my plans out of my mind. But the power of my will or consciousness stops there . . . There is a moment when sleep 'comes', settling on this imitation of itself which I have been offering to it, and I succeed in becoming what I was trying to be: an unseeing and almost unthinking mass, riveted to a point in space and in the world henceforth only through the anonymous alertness of the senses. (Ph.P p. 164–5; PP p. 191).

Sleeping gives us a paradigm of bodily withdrawal. First the withdrawal is initiated by a posturing. The sleeper assumes the position of sleep as the girl's muteness began by withdrawing from articulation. This posture alone is not enough to bring about situational withdrawal. The positioning is offered to the capacity of the body-subject to withdraw projects and assume an anonymity in withdrawal. Consequently, the projects associated with this part or parts of the body-subject recede into the attitude of the body-subject before it fixes upon some object or goal, that is they recede into a general attitude, frozen from involvement. "In the case of the girl just discussed, the move towards the future, towards the living present or towards the past, the power of learning, of maturing, of entering into communication with others, have become, as it were, arrested in a bodily symptom, existence is tied up and the body has become 'the place where life hides away.' " (Ph.P p. 164; PP p. 192) Secondly, as in sleep, the withdrawal of the body is not an irretrievable withdrawal from the world, but a withdrawal into a general attitude which, without any reference to detail, comprehensively avoids all experiences which might be associated with that bodily-project. Even so, the sleeper may be awakened, or as he states apropos of the case study mentioned above, the girl can recover her voice through a bodily conversion which amounts to recalling a forgotten and "genuine gesture." (Ph. P. p. 165; PP p. 192) In other words, the recovery of a shutting off from the world entails being in a situation which allows one to respond, in a "gestural manner," with one's body in a way which can freshly reopen some part of the world which has been lost to it. (We might note that Merleau-Ponty's work here predates the psychotherapeutic approaches of Jacques Lacan who saw cure coming to his patients when they initiated a gesture which reopened the fearful or distrusting parts of their past).

Can one speak of authenticity in relation to the body-subject? Merleau-Ponty states of the sleeper and the case history mentioned above "We remain free in relation to sleep and sickness to the exact extent to which we remain always involved in the waking and healthy state." (Ph.P p. 164; PP p. 191). Authenticity does not require the acknowledgement of absolute choice (Sartre), nor a resolve to one's involvement that entails an acceptance of one's "being-towards-death" (Heidegger). Merleau-Ponty, in several passages in *The Phenomenology* states there is a "pulse of my existence," a "systole and diastole." (Ph.P pp. 164, 285; PP p. 192, 330) The metaphor of systole and diastole, the contraction and dilation of the heart, expresses an "existential pulse" of contraction and dilation within a situation. The retreat from a specific situation into an "anonymous life which subtends my personal one" (Ph.P p. 165; PP p. 192) is part of the human lot. It is the role of the body to insure both these movements. Thus pulse marks the rhythm of the body-subject as it recurrently shifts from a general directedness toward the perceptual horizons to an emergence in relation to some object. The notion of inauthenticity for Merleau-Ponty amounts to a severance from this rhythm or pulse. The metaphor of sleep is again helpful. A freezing of an already established body-project from the rhythm of existence counts as a variety of inauthenticity. Its earmarks are a retreat into a generalized existence which neither allows for nor discards a project. The girl who has withdrawn her power of speech is disadvantaged because she can neither disavow her situation nor accept it. To summarize, for Merleau-Ponty the issues of authenticity and inauthenticity, if these terms may be applied at all, concern the manner in which the world may be zoned off or expended; they do not involve taking a stand on an involvement. Like perception itself, fundamentally these issues rest in the manner in which the body returns to involvement from a submergence in the general anonymity of the body. To speak of a committed individual is only sensible if one can also refer to orientations or projects which the individual can own much in the same way that he can own that the moon looks bigger on the horizon than overhead. It is not a question of resolve or decision-making, but an opportunity for vitality which is offered to us as bodily beings, and which, if we do not descend into lack of corporeal action or reaction, allows us to have more of a world.

Notes To Chapter Two

[1] For Heidegger's use of saying as "way-making", see for example *On the Way to Language*, Harper and Row, New York, 1971, p. 108.

[2] Heidegger, M. *The Origin of the Work of Art* as reprinted in *Poetry, Language and Thought* translated by A. Hofstadter, Harper & Row, New York, 1971, p. 22.

[3] Ibid. p. 24.

[4] Ibid. p. 25.

[5] Ibid. p. 26.

[6] Cf. Dreyfus, H. L., *Husserl's Phenomenology of Perception: from Transcendental to Existential Phenomenology*, p. 89

[7] Heidegger, op. cit. p. 26.

[8] For a Heideggerian account of the subject/object ontology and the remarkably broad legacy of ontological confusions which follow from it see in particular Heidegger's "The Age of the World Picture" as published in *The Question Concerning Technology and Other Essays*, Harper and Row, New York, 1977.

[9] Hamlyn, D. W., *Sensation and Perception, a History of the Philosophy of Perception*, The Humanities Press, London, 1960, p. 186.

[10] Nietzsche, *Thus Spake Zarathustra*, Part I, Section 4, T. Common translation, Modern Library Edition, New York, 1927, p. 33.

[11] Marcel, Gabriel, *Metaphysical Journal*, Chicago, Henry Rennery Co., translation by Wall, see pages 332–9.

[12] Bergson, Henri, *Matter and Memory*, Doubleday, 1959, pp. 1–6.

[13] Sartre, Jean-Paul, *Being and Nothingness* Washington Square Press, Barnes translation, 1968, pp. 401–460.

[14] Foucault, *Discipline and Punish: The Birth of the Prison*. Alan Sheridan translation. Vintage/Random House. 1979, New York, See Chapter 7 in general for Foucault's development of "disciplinary power" as a means for bodily readiness for a variety of social reforms.

[15] Plato, "The Meno", *The Dialogues of Plato*, Jowett translation, Stephanus page 75b, In Random House Edition, 1937, N. Y., p. 354.

[16] Samuel Mallin informatively makes the point in his discussion of Merleau-Ponty's account of color constancy that Merleau-Ponty uncovers the sensibility in existential writers use of lighting as an ontological metaphor. He states: "We can see now that the light analogy that existentialists favor for describing Existence and its field has much ontological truth and is not as ill-chosen as many commentators make it out to be." (Mallin, Samuel, *Merleau-Ponty's Philosophy* New Haven, Yale University Press, 1979, p. 155.) This point is well taken and unravels some of Merleau-Ponty's own statements. For example, in one of the more difficult passages in *The Phenomenology*, Merleau-Ponty designates a "light which bursts forth" in the dehiscence of "self to self" (Ph.P p. 426; PP p. 487). Lighting as a level, by which we see, becomes an apt ontological metaphor insofar as a "light which bursts forth" can count as the initiation of a new and fundamental way of conceiving of our world, cf. a neutral level according to which we see.

[17] Lessing, Doris, *The Golden Note-book*, Ballantine Books, New York, 1968, p. 613.

[18] The terms "interior and exterior horizons" are used often by Merleau-Ponty. In this case his usage agrees with Husserl's in whose writings they are fundamental terms. "Exterior horizon" indicates main features of the perceptual field. The term entails that the perceptual field extends outward from a perceiving subject in increasing indeterminacy. The field, as the horizon, has no fixed limit. It is assumed that there are areas of varying determinacy which proceed finally until there is only a "general form of the world." "Interior horizon" applies to some particular thing and indicates that the hidden sides or interiors also are "there" but indeterminate. Again, the notion implies that the possibility of investigation of the thing has not specific terminus; it permits endless exploration. See for example Husserl's *Erfarhrung und Urteil*, Prague, Academia Verlagsbuchhandlung, 1939, p. 172 for Husserl's characteristic use of these terms.

[19] Merleau-Ponty refers to the body's power to retain a repertory of skills as the "I can" (*je peux*) aspect of the body-subject. See for example Ph.P p. 137; PP p. 160. He states he has imported this designation from Husserl's unpublished writings. Again we confront the pattern wherein Merleau-Ponty identifies his view with Husserl at the expense of his presenting his own position. For Merleau-Ponty, as we have seen the body-subject is not a personal subject. Personal identity arises in the manner in which an interpenetration occurs between the social and natural worlds. If one should give a formula to the body-subject as the retainer of projects one ought not to speak of an "I" or an "it" for that manner. But speaking of an "on peux" which we would at least consistent with Merleau-Ponty thought no longer allows Merleau-Ponty to find his own innovations (inappropriately) in Husserl.

3

The Foundations of Language and Reflection

> The relation of reason to fact, or eternity to time, like that of reflection to the unreflective, of thought to language or of thought to perception is this two-way relationship that phenomenology has called *Fundierung*: the founding term, or originator—time, the unreflective, the fact, language, perception—is primary in the sense that the originated is presented as a determinate or explicit form of the originator, which prevents the latter from reabsorbing the former, and yet the originator is not primary in the empiricist sense and the originated is not simply derived from it, since it is through the originated that the originator is made manifest. (Ph.P, p. 394; PP p. 451)

1. Merleau-Ponty's revision of Husserl's *Fundierung* relation

The quote above expresses the weight that Merleau-Ponty gives to Husserl's concept of *Fundierung*. In this section, I will be arguing that the notion of *Fundierung* is elemental to Merleau-Ponty's way of conceiving the relationship of the body to cognition, language and the social world. We shall spend most of our time considering the role of the body to language as an expression of the *Fundierung* relationship. The relation of the body to cognition and Merleau-Ponty's notion of "radical reflection" will be discussed in less detail. But many of the claims made about language may be applied *mutatis mutandis* to cognition and reflection.

Husserl presents a definition of the *Fundierung* relation in the *Logische Untersuchunge*n, Part Three, Section 14. It appears as

95

a technical term and occurs repeatedly throughout the rest of the treatise. Let us consider two particularly significant parts of his presentation. First the definition of *Fundierung*:[1]

> If a law of essence means that an A cannot as such exist except in a more comprehensive unity which associates it with an M, we say that an A *as such requires foundation by an M* or also that *an A as such needs to be supplemented by an M*. [Husserl's emphasis]

To understand Husserl's definition quoted above, we need consider some elemental concepts Husserl proposes in this Part and which he maintains as technical terms. First the notion of *pieces*. Pieces are independent parts. They are parts that can be presented separately from the wholes which contain them. In a bed, the mattress and frame are pieces because they can be presented separately. *Moments*, on the other hand, are non-independent parts. They cannot be presented separately from other wholes or parts. Thus, hue and brightness, for example, are moments of color.

Husserl also distinguishes reciprocal from one-sided foundational relations. As the terms imply, in reciprocal foundational relations, the parts "interpenetrate;" one part is supplementary to the existence of the other and *vice versa*. In one-sided foundational relations, such as the relation, for Husserl, between judgment and perception, judgments are non-independent upon percepts, whereas, in Husserl's view, perception is independent from judgments. Alice, in *perceiving* a rabbit, may ordinarily not come to a judgment about it. But the Alice of Carroll's story who *judges* the rabbit as late depends upon her perception.

Husserl tells us that what is particularly unique about his definition of foundation is that it does not entail additional concepts, ideas or syntheses which unify parts. By allowing that parts may interpenetrate without having to supply a conceptual apparatus which subsumes or synthesizes the parts, Husserl frees his investigations from a good deal of the conceptual baggage of the neo-Kantianism which dominated the researches of his contemporaries. As he states[2] in the case of moments, we have parts which

> are in fact "founded" on one another, and for this reason they require no chains or bonds to chain or knit them together, or to bring them to one another. In their case all these expressions have in fact no sense at all. Where it makes nonsense to speak of isolation, the problem of overcoming such isolation is also nonsensical.

As indicated earlier, Husserl returns to the notion of foundation throughout the *Logical Investigations*. Nor is it given up in his later writings. His understanding of judgments and their relation to "substrates" in his later logical work, *Formal and Transcendental Logic* reiterates the same distinction.[3] Now, I would like to point out a second main feature of this notion as Husserl presents it in the *Logical Investigations*. It is this feature of the *Fundierung* relation which in fact illuminates main developments of Merleau-Ponty's writings from the *Phenomenology of Perception* onward. In section 21 of Part III, Husserl sets about to define the notion of whole *by way of the notion of foundation*. He states[4]

> If all is taken thus generally, one could then give the following noteworthy definition of the *pregnant concept of Whole* by way of the *notion of Foundation*:
>
> By a Whole we understand a range of contents which are all covered *by a single foundation* without the help of further contents. [Husserl's emphasis]

The abstraction of Husserl's language ought not to hide from us that Husserl offers an innovation in conceiving of "wholes" in general. He is holding that a whole may be analyzed via the concept of *Fundierung*. The move that Husserl has made here sets up a line of inquiry which takes a relation of parts as basic and the existence of wholes as derivative. Is this a return to the "objective world" which would deny the significance of the physiognomies of perceptual "wholes?" Quite clearly not. It is

97

rather a way of analyzing anything that might come before consciousness as a network of relations of parts which, given the requisite version of the *Fundierung* relation, become "wholes" not through association or combination of parts as the traditional empiricist would hold, but through "moments" which supplement other "moments," that is through an interpenetration of parts which are "non-independent."

As we have seen in the quote at the head of this section, Merleau-Ponty finds the *Fundierung* relation descriptive of a great array of issues. He mentions the relation of reason to fact, eternity to time, reflection to the unreflective, thought to language and thought to perception. He claims here that our world, which may be approached conceptually via the regions specified, actually involves an interdependency of parts. We are engaging in fruitless lines of inquiry if we inquire into the ways in which language and perception interrelate if we assume that they can be isolated from each other. They are not parts unified by a whole. They are non-independent from each other and what we know of the final result is just this interpenetration. Merleau-Ponty, in fact, reshapes Husserl's notion by conceiving of reciprocal moments along the lines of structures or fields. In his view the parts in the *Fundierung* relation have the following features:

1) The parts may themselves be structures or fields, e. g. lighting as such might be called "part" of our world having its own structure and manners of equilibrium.

2) The parts, as fields or structures, are "supplemented by" i.e. *founded in* other fields or structures, but in principle one field does not absorb another.

3) There is an overall tendency towards integration within the interdependent structures or fields which leads one field to maintain a "mapping" on each other field. This integration of fields, which is always to some extent unsuccessful is maintained by the body-subject.

Although Merleau-Ponty explicitly alludes to the *Fundierung* relation as elemental to his understanding of how our world is rooted in perception, it is important for us to see that despite his allusions, Merleau-Ponty's view is not Husserl's. For Husserl all our experience is finally a moment of—it is *founded* in—transcendental subjectivity. For Merleau-Ponty, on the other hand, transcendental subjectivity mistakenly implies that we could radically disinvolve ourselves from the world. In spite of the great value Merleau-Ponty attributes to Husserl's work, he never allows the possibility of the disengagement from the natural attitude which a reduction to transcendental subjectivity requires. Merleau-Ponty changes Husserl's notion of *Fundierung* in a way that is similar to the way that Sartre reforms Husserl's notion of intentionality. In *The Transcendence of the Ego* Sartre argues that a Transcendental Ego is not needed in the intentional analysis of consciousness. One can speak of intentions apart from an ''ego-pole'' from which they emanate. Merleau-Ponty, already by the time of the writing of *The Structure of Behavior*, has rejected a notion of intentionality which would be limited to act-intentionality, but, in a reform which is similar to Sartre's elimination of the transcendental ego, he holds that it is enough to have a collation of parts, where ''parts'' here is expanded to the notion of fields or structures. There is no need to suppose an overriding field i. e. a field of transcendental consciousness. There is a teleology to our attempts to integrate parts of our world, wherein we set about increasingly to concatenate fields. But this directedness is always incomplete and observes no overall field as Husserl supposed.

2. The interpenetration of the body and language

The denomination of objects does not follow upon recognition; it is itself recognition. . . The word bears the meaning, and, by imposing it on the object, I am conscious of reaching that object. (Ph. P. p. 177; PP p. 207)

It is my body which gives significance not only to natural objects but also to cultural objects like words. (Ph.P p. 235; PP p. 272)

The two quotes that I cite above seem to offer two very different approaches to the language/world relation. On the one hand, Merleau-Ponty is holding that the word ''imposes meaning on the object." But as stated in the second quote, we are offered the view that an object is given its verbal significance through the meaning which is extended to it by the body. Actually it is a strength of Merleau-Ponty's view that both accounts are held to be elemental to the world/language relation. In Husserlian terminology they are in reciprocal foundational relation. Both parts create a whole, and the nature of the whole may be understood by a consideration of the structures involved and the manner in which they interpenetrate.

Let us consider this manner of approaching the language/world relation by looking at views which would purportedly account for language as an extension of gesture. We shall make a short excursion and consider some phonetic correlates that we find in a great variety of languages. If we look, for example, at the way that spatial relations are expressed in several European and Asian languages, we find that there is a correlation between movements of articulation in the mouth and spatial relations. The synonyms for "before" are expressed forward in the mouth; whereas the words for behind involve a pulling of the vocal organs backwards. We might note that we can find the same relation if we look through a multi-lingual list of words for "front" and "back." See the list below for a tabulating of multi-lingual synonyms for "before" and "behind."

Language	'Before'	'Behind'
French	devant	derriere
Italian	devanti a	dietro
Spanish	delante de	detras de
German	vor	hinter
Dutch	voor	hinter
Danish	foran	bag
Russian	pered	szadi
Polish	przed	za
Czech	pred	za
Hungarian	elott	mogott
Finnish	edessa	takana

Language	'Before'	'Behind'
Estonian	ees	taga
Turkish	onde	arkada
Arabic	oddam	wara
Japanese	mae	ushiro
Korean	ap	twi
Chinese	ch'ien mien	hou-pien

To clarify how mouth positions reflect positions in space we need to very briefly review some elements of phonetics. According to basic phonetics, consonants may be divided according to whether they are "plosives" or "continuants" and according to whether they are labial, dental or guttural. The first division trades upon the fact that in the consonants n, m, ng, s, z, f, v, h, sh, and the soft g there is no stoppage of air flow. Air from the lungs is allowed to pass through the mouth over the tongue only shaped by the vocal organs and not obstructed by them. On the other hand with plosives, such as t, d, ch, j, p, b, and the hard g, there is an instant when the air flow is stopped. As the term implies a small explosion of air is involved in the sounding of these consonants. The second division between labials, dentals, and gutturals distinguishes the part of the mouth which forms the consonant. Labials are made with the lips; dentals, with the tongue behind the front teeth; and gutturals with the tongue at the back of the soft palate.

Within this first list of multi-lingual synonyms we notice that without exception the words for "before" are more forward in the mouth than the word for "behind". Not an absolute, but a relative positioning is involved. The word for "before" cannot be found always to involve labials, although labials are much more common to this list than in the list of words for "behind," but if one compares the relative position in the mouth case by case the position of the vocal organs reflects the before/behind spatial relation.

Let us look at another example. This next list reflects the "continuant" versus "plosive" distinction. See list below. Here

we will look at cognates for "sea" and "earth" or "ground."
Now it is not spatial position which is presented in microcosm in
the mouth but cognate bodily movement. The sea as we move
over or through it does not involve an obstruction of movement;
whereas the earth or ground, at least insofar as it breaks a fall,
always does. Accordingly, the words for sea depend on continuant consonants; the words for earth or ground employ plosives.

Language	'Sea'	'Earth,' or 'Ground'
French	mer	terre
Italian	mare	terra
Spanish	mer	tierra
German	meer	Erde
Dutch	zee	aarde
Russian	more	potshva
Polish	morze	gleba
Czech	more	puda
Lithuanian	jura	padas
Latvian	jura	augsne
Turkish	deniz	toprak
Arabic	bahar	trab
Japanese	umi	dai chi
Korean	hoswu	taeji
Chinese	hoi	tati

Here the variation is remarkably correlative. The words for
"sea" all involve only continuants with the apparent exception
of Turkish and Arabic. But these languages are not actual
exceptions since, in comparison to the words for "earth" in
these languages, the words for sea are relatively less plosive.

How are we to interpret such correlations which seem to make
the actions of vocal organs into a microcosm of the way the body
relates to its environs?

The observation that the movements made in vocal articulation match bodily gestures arises as early as Plato's *Cratylus*.[5]
Commentators have pointed out that the etymologies that Plato

offers in this dialogue were probably not meant to be taken seriously. But that he did seriously entertain the view that names were correlates of bodily gestures is not doubted. Darwin also explores the view that vocal movements are correlative to bodily movements in *The Expression of the Emotions*.[6] He considers a "sympathy" that exists between bodily gestures and vocal expression. A particularly developed account of the expression of the relationship between bodily movement and the movement of organs of speech was offered by Richard Paget in his study, *Human Speech*. I will quote Paget's colorful expression of the manner in which he conceives the relation between vocal and bodily expression:[7]

> Originally man expressed his ideas by gesture, but as he gesticulated with his hands, his tongues, lips and jaw unconsciously followed suit in a ridiculous fashion, "understudying" the action of the hands. The consequence was that when, owing to pressure of other business, the principal actors (the hands) retired from the stage—as much as principal actors ever do—their understudies—the tongue, lips and jaw—were already proficient in the pantomimic art.
>
> Then the great discovery was made that if while making a gesture with the tongue and lips, air was blown through the oral or nasal cavities, the gesture became audible as a whispered speech sound. If, while pantomiming with tongue, lips and jaw our ancestors sang, roared or grunted—in order to draw attention to what they were doing—a still louder and more remarkable effect was produced, namely that which we call voiced speech.

Paget's presentation of the "pantomimic" view of speech is remarkably detailed. Paget goes so far as to propose the notion a "tongue track", which enables him to map out the main moves of the tongue in the articulation of a word. He finds in this mapping that thematic bodily moves which are implied by the word are recaptured in pantomime by the tongue. The fundamental sound of "agh" or "angh" involves a contraction of the throat in its expression. So it pantomimes choking or strangling and appears in words such as "anger". The root syllable "an" or "en" on the other hand involves an freer flow of air which is nasalized. It is characteristically found in words which reflect upon breathing or the wind. Examples here, among many others, include the Greek *anemos* (wind) and the German *atmen* (to breathe).

Now Merleau-Ponty's account of the body-subject allows for a sophisticated approach to the role of gestural elements in language. The body, in Merleau-Ponty's view, operates according to a *schema corporel*. The body-subject transfers bodily actions from the fingers to the hands or feet. If one can write one's name on paper, one can write it in the air with one's hand or with one's toe on sand. The body provides its own system of equivalents given degrees of dexterity and awkwardness. But even among awkward or unpracticed movements we admit the rough sketching of movements which we might express through other parts of the body. Thus it is not surprising as the gesture theory of language would suppose that bodily movement may find translation to the movements of the tongue or throat. This is the sense of Merleau-Ponty's assent to the gesture theory in saying:

> The spoken word is a genuine gesture, and it contains its meaning in the same way as the gesture does. (Ph.P. p. 183; PP p. 214)

The gesture theory offered by Paget and sketched as early as Plato, however, clearly has little validity in the case of words that not are related to highly concrete actions. Correlations exist between words such as "kick", "hit", "strike" and "knock" and the acts that they refer to which involve a collision or breaking of the flow of action. And it is clear that other words which suggest a greater degree of fluidity of action such as "move" or "merge" roughly accord with what we would expect from the gestural significance implied by continuants. But it is also clear that if one tried to explain the phonetics of naming in general according to gestural significance, one would greatly overstate the relation. It is not only that most terms do not imply any concrete action and thereby are irrelevant to questions of gesture, not to mention pantomime. Even when some agreement is observed between the term and the bodily movement, the words themselves admit much more variation and difference than the bodily actions suggest. If we consider some of the examples mentioned, "kicking," with two guttural plosives fits the collision in bodily forces implied. But "punting" depends upon a reference to the rules of football for its significance. At best bodily correlates can enliven these terms with rough gestural value; they can hardly account for their differences.

The problem with the gestural view of language is that it endorses the view that the body is important in understanding how words are given significance, but it sees the role of the body as limited to the body which you and I observe, that is the phenomenal body. It misses the notion of the body as a repository of body projects; it misses the sense of the body as a "je peux." The relationship between the body, as rooted in the world, and language is one of interpenetration. The body catches onto the speech which surrounds it. Consequently bodily involvements and language are "moments" of each other. Speech is not meaningful without its interpenetration into human projects; and on the other hand, human projects are shaped and questioned—in general take their place—in language.

3. The foundation of language in the body: neither sublimation nor reduction

A story is told in a children's book of the disappointment of a small boy who put on his grandmother's spectacles and took up her book in the expectation of being able to find in it the stories which she used to tell him. The tale ends with these words: "Well, what a fraud! Where's the story? I can see nothing but black and white." For the child the "story" and the thing expressed are not "ideas" or meanings" nor are speaking or reading "intellectual operations". The story is a world which there must be some way of magically calling up by putting on spectacles and leaning over a book. The power possessed by language of bringing the thing expressed into existence, of opening up to thought new ways, new dimensions, new landscapes is, in the last analysis, as obscure for the adult as for the child. (Ph. P. p. 401; PP p. 459–60)

Samuel B. Mallin's recent study of Merleau-Ponty's writings, *Merleau-Ponty's Philosophy*, Yale U. Press, 1979, which contributes to scholarship on Merleau-Ponty by organizing his thought in such a way that it may be seen in its consistency throughout recurrent topics such as situations, perceptual parameters, evidence and truth, suffers in its presentation of language by emphasizing notion of sublimation. Merleau-Ponty often employs the term sublimation,[8] but when he does employ the notion of sublimation he characteristically suggests that it is only one way of looking at a reciprocal foundational relation. The notion of sublimation is in itself inadequate to express the relation. That Mallin uses the notion of sublimation, thematically, to discuss language reflects a tendency to perceive Merleau-Ponty's view of language—one might include cognition, reflection, or temporality here as well—as fundamentally *reducible* to bodily projects. The language he employs recaptures and reinstates this line of thought.[9]

To be sure, in a statement which might be taken as a motto for *The Phenomenology of Perception*, Merleau-Ponty states: "All consciousness is, in some measure, perceptual consciousness." (Ph. P. p. 395; PP p. 452) But this statement does not entail that all consciousness may be reduced to perceptual consciousness. It is certainly a large part of Merleau-Ponty's general project in the *Phenomenology of Perception* to show how many topics which ordinarily make up the mainstay of philosophical concern leave out the role of the body/perceptual world system. The centrality which Merleau-Ponty gives to the body/perceptual world system often yields a misreading which I will call the sublimation/reduction misreading of *The Phenomenology of Perception*. In the first error, one reduces the complexity of linguistic or cognitive structures to bodily activities. In the second error, conversely, one tends to see language and cognition as a sublimation of bodily activities. Neither position represents Merleau-Ponty's view. They both depend upon a misreading of Merleau-Ponty's sense of reciprocal foundation.

At the period of the writing of the *Phenomenology of Perception*, Merleau-Ponty thinks of language in terms of Gestalt theory, albeit with the revisions he brings to Gestalt theory. As he states in an essay written at this period: "Language must surround each speaking subject, like an instrument with its own inertia, its own demands, constraints and internal logic." (SNS, p. 87; *SNS* p. 153). He continues to view language as a Gestalt in the period which follows *The Phenomenology*. He states for example in notes collected from courses given at the Sorbonne from 1949 to 1951 under the title *Consciousness and the Acquisition of Language*:

> In truth, a language is not made up of *words*, each of which is endowed with one or several meanings. Each word has its meaning only inasmuch as it is sustained in this signification by all the others. The same holds true for these others. The only reality is the *Gestalt* of language. (p. 92)

As has been pointed out by Silverman among others, Merleau-Ponty at the time of the writing of *The Phenomenology* had not yet incorporated Saussure's understanding of linguistic systems into his view.[10] But even after he accepts Saussure's position, Merleau-Ponty still thinks of language as a Gestalt. His endorsing of the Saussurian account, which we find from lecture notes dating from 1947 onwards, is prepared previously through his understanding language to be a Gestalt. In fact already in *The Phenomenology* he maintains that the special peculiarity of language as compared to other forms of expression is that speech "seems able to detach itself from material instruments" (Ph.P p. 391; PP p. 448). Hence in *The Phenomenology* he is already close to the Saussurian account and goes so far as to affirm that language finally only makes sense by its manner of referring to itself. As he states:

> . . . in fact, as we have said, the clearness of language stands out from an obscure background, and if we carry our research far enough we shall find that language is equally uncommunicative of anything other than itself, that its meaning is inseparable from it. (Ph.P p. 188; PP p. 219)

Let us be more specific. For Merleau-Ponty, Saussure's "diacritical" theory of language furthers basic claims he had already brought to the subject in *The Phenomenology*. In Saussure's view, each word takes on significance through establishing how it differs from other usages.[11] "Monday" is sensible because of the difference it marks from "Tuesday". Like the stones that make up the Roman Arch, each word holds its place by view of the positions it stands in relation to others. The days of the week, just because they express and are fundamentally differences from other days in the sequence that make up the week, suggest a relation to other terms. Thus language as "diacritical"—Saussure's manner of expressing language as a system of differences—provides the important concepts of meaning as "difference" but it also is in keeping with the view offered in *The Phenomenology* which is indicated by the quote above, that is that the meaning of language depends upon its manner of referring to itself.

There are important differences between Merleau-Ponty's and Saussure's accounts. Merleau-Ponty, unlike Saussure offers the notion of "authentic expression." Language as a systematic sedimentation of meanings is the received coinage which "makes up the general run of empirical language." (Ph. P. p. 178n; PP p. 207n) Although it comprises the established background of linguistic usages, it is still "second order expression." (Ph P. p. 178n; PP p. 207n) But, we are not only privy to an acquired system of significances through language. The system itself as a depository of acquired or "sedimented" expressions contains expressions which at one time were freshly acquired. In *Consciousness and the Acquisition of Language* we have examples drawn from the development of Latin to French.[12] The changes for example from the Latin "utus" suffix in words such as *absolutus* to the French *absolu* occurred in a manner which indicates that there was a systemic shifting in Latin which respected whole regions of its syntax. What is described here syntactically has its semantic analogue. The formation of a new distinction—the birth of a new expression—accords with a resetting of relations within the system of language. And since language is founded in the world and *vice versa*, a shift in the usage of language means an initiation into a new manner of approaching the world. *Authentic speech* is this sort of speech which inaugurates new manners of approaching the world. The very possibility of authentic speech gives language the capacity for establishing new meaning which would surpass established significances.

Conceiving language as a system which is "uncommunicative of anything other than itself," does not suggest a view where language may be reduced to bodily projects. To be sure, the body catches onto linguistic expressions making these projects "non-independent" from language. This means that henceforth it will be nonsense to speak of some projects which are not linguistic. Promise-making, for example, is necessarily linguistic but it also expresses projects and intentions which are maintained by the body. Our worldly involvements, as well as our dreams or hallucinations are "shot through" with language to the extent that we cannot admit something to our social world until we can, in principle, name it. But there is no question of the possibility of a reduction to bodily projects. As he states: "It has always been observed that speech or gesture transfigure the body." (Ph.P. p. 197; PP p. 230)

Merleau-Ponty's account of how the body avails itself of linguistic usage is modelled on catching onto the significance of a tool:

> On day I "caught on" to the word "sleet," much as one imitates a gesture . . . The word has never been inspected, analyzed, known and constituted, but caught and taken up by a power of speech and, in the last analysis, by a motor power given to me along with the first experience I have of my body and its perceptual and practical fields. (Ph.P. p. 403; PP p. 461)

The "penetration" of the body into linguistic usage entails that language is dependent upon its involvement with body-projects. The presence that language has, before we have caught onto a usage, is much like our experience of a social world which we have not found our place. Merleau-Ponty's description of an alien social world matches how language appears before its usages have been "caught onto:"

> If it is a question of an unknown or alien civilization, then several manners of being or of living can find their place in the ruins or in the broken instruments which I discover, or in the landscape through which I roam. The cultural world is then ambiguous, but it is already present. I have before me a society to be known. (Ph.P. p. 348; PP p. 400)

In the citation which heads this section, a child puts on his grandmother's spectacles but cannot find the story the grandmother reads. "Where is the story?" he states. "I can see nothing but black and white." In terms of our overview, the child cannot find the story because he has not caught onto the cyphers with his body. But this does not imply the story is an extension of bodily projects alone. The power withheld from the child opens up to thought "new ways, new dimensions, new landscapes." The penetration between language and body-projects is reciprocal.

Far from language being based or built out of bodily projects, then, language, as conceived as founded in the body and *vice versa,* allows, through the peculiarities of language, an inauguration into cognition and reflection. We may sum up Merleau-Ponty's view on language by the following statements:

1. Language comprises a system or Gestalt.

2. This Gestalt has the peculiarity of offering significances which are *qua* significances detached from the vehicle or apparatus which conveys the expression.

3. Language as a Gestalt interpenetrates with the other fields that comprise our lived world; there is a more or less successful mapping of one structure upon another.

4. A new structuring or ordering within the linguistic Gestalt reflects a shift in comprehension of the world. This shift, with its resultant institutionalizing of a new linguistic usage, is a case of "authentic speech."

It is important for us to see, that given his revision of the *Fundierung* relation, at no point is it sensible from Merleau-Ponty's point of view to speak of pure reflection or thought, any more than it is possible to speak of linguistic significances which have no reference to the world which we inhabit with our bodies. But on the other hand, language and reflection as structures privileged through the capacity of language to reflect upon itself allows for a "teleology of consciousness" towards which our bodily projects may follow and from which they may take their meaning. Although the interpenetration of language and the natural world is never complete, their reciprocal founding creates a world which is in principle nameable at the same time it creates a world which is an arena for verbal gestures wherein the verbal gestures *are* the enactment of projects. Linguistic gestures are on the horizon of every perception; they are "on the same footing as color and form." (Ph.P. p. 178; PP p. 207)

One more word about language and the *Fundierung* relation for Merleau-Ponty. There are many correspondences between Merleau-Ponty's approach to language and Heidegger's later approach. As we have indicated, Merleau-Ponty holds that language has the peculiarity of being wholly about itself. Heidegger also makes this position thematic to his approach to language in essays collected under the title *On the Way to Language*. Heidegger begins an essay entitled, "The Way to Language", for example, with a quote from Novalis which states that language is wholly concerned with itself. As he begins:[13]

The peculiar property of language, namely that language is concerned exclusively with itself—precisely that is known to no one.

Heidegger's approach at least in the period of the writing of these essays on language depends upon his reinterpretation of the hermeneutical circle. Heidegger's later view, in this reinterpretation, corresponds to Merleau-Ponty's in that both thinkers admit a manner of authentic speech. Heidegger's understanding of authentic speech is not discussed in terms of shifts of a system which is "reorganized under a fresh law"

(Ph.P p. 194; PP p. 226). Nonetheless Heidegger, in speaking of "authentic saying"[14] touches upon a similar issue. If language is about itself, then in what way can we speak of changes that come about in language through acquired significances. We cannot fall back upon a hermeneutic circle since the circle itself shifts as language shifts. To explain authentic saying, Heidegger returns to his key notions of unconcealment and Appropriation. But in so doing he concords with the notion that language, as authentic speech, captures freshly and fundamentally new significances. But we ought not to overlook that the acceptance of a foundational relation in language is a main difference between Merleau-Ponty's view and Heidegger's. Again it is a question of the founding of language in the body. And again this does not imply that language is causally related to bodily projects, but that for a linguistic significance to make sense, it must be reciprocally interrelated with bodily projects. This line of thinking is fundamentally different from Heidegger's view.

4. Radical reflection is not adduced by a disinvolved subject

Reflection then does not itself grasp its significance unless it refers to the unreflective fund of experiences which it presupposes, upon which it draws, and which constitutes for it a kind of original past, a past which has never been present. (Ph.P. p. 242; PP p. 280)

Reflection cannot be thorough-going, or bring to complete elucidation of its object, if it does not arrive at awareness of itself as well as of its results. We must not only adopt a reflective attitude in an impregnable *Cogito*, but furthermore reflect upon this reflection, understand the natural situation which it is conscious of succeeding and which is therefore part of its definition; not merely practice philosophy, but realize the transformation which it brings with it in the spectacle of the world and in our existence . . . The core of philosophy is no longer an autonomous transcendental subjectivity, to be found everywhere and nowhere: it lies in the perpetual beginning of philosophy, at the point where an individual life begins to reflect on itself. (Ph.P. p. 62; PP p. 75)

The above quotes are from the few passages in the *Phenomenology of Perception* where Merleau-Ponty refers to his notion of "radical reflection," the form of philosophizing which he calls a main theme of "radical self-discovery" and which he claims contemporary philosophy is "attempting to achieve."[15] (Ph. P. p. 62; PP p. 75) Earlier commentators, for example, Ballard[16] have voiced criticism which would take strong objection to Merleau-Ponty's account of radical reflection. De Waelhens alludes to the critics of this issue. As he states:[17]

> We need finally to meet a last and particularly grave objection which certain critics find decisive, and which would be such, if, in effect, truly founded. This objection contests the possibility of defining perception in the manner that Merleau-Ponty does and at the same time of writing a phenomenology of it. This manner of treating perception supposes, from abundant evidence, a reflection or a return of the perceiving subject upon himself. Where this return and eidetic view [vue eidétique] of the nature and essence of perception towards which it is directed supposes a detachment in regards to perception and a capacity to survey it. But this description of the perceiving subject, such as Merleau-Ponty presents it, is precisely what he contests and forbids.

I state de Waelhens' expression of criticism of Merleau-Ponty's approach, which was published as early as 1951, because it hits directly upon what would seem to be a basic inconsistency in Merleau-Ponty's thought. In my opinion early critics justifiably criticized Merleau-Ponty's method. Not because it did involve a detached reflection—detachment and the capacity to survey the phenomenological field is not possible for an engaged body-subject—but because of the confusion that arises by expressing his own method of philosophizing in the language of Husserlian phenomenology. As such the innovation of his approach was easily confused with Husserl's.

Merleau-Ponty was engaged in formulating his own concept of philosophizing and employed the language of reflection to do so. The use of the term "reflection" itself did not help. With its suggestion of unbiased mirroring, it implies a reflective subject whose nature does not change the spectacle. Again, we have a case of one of Merleau-Ponty's own views which is offered in Husserlian language and which in effect misrepresents both Husserl as well as himself. The objections which de Waehlens

cites, if not applicable to Merleau-Ponty's actual view, at least
had the justification of rightly questioning a point of view which
was burdened by models and terminology suggesting an idealized spectator. It is not surprising that Merleau-Ponty finally
changed his language and in his last work invented his own way
of speaking of his understanding of philosophy. In *The Visible
and the Invisible*, he chooses to describe the philosophical
questioning he is interested in as "question-knowing". (VI p.
129; *VI* p. 171)

In the first quote cited at the head of this chapter, Merleau-
Ponty indicates that radical reflection "draws upon" an
unreflected fund of experience." He calls this an "original past,
a past which has never been a present." What is the original past
he refers to here? His basing temporal dimensions on an original
past leads him to depart from both Husserl's and Heidegger's
view of temporality. For Merleau-Ponty, there is a background
sense of time which is entailed by our having a world. As he
states: ". . . this primordial temporality is not a juxtaposition of
external events since it is the power which holds them together
while keeping them apart." (Ph.P p. 422; PP p. 483) The past,
present and future can be read as such in relationship to this
"primordial" time which is already there. To have a future we
need to consider some moment as a point of departure; to have
a past we need to consider a moment as a point of arrival. But
both arrival and departure are implicated in the more primitive
sense of time. We experience a moment "in time" as we say.
Merleau-Ponty alludes to Heidegger's notion of interpretation as
an "as-structure" (See *Being and Time*, Section 32) for a way of
understanding the temporal dimensions of past, present, and
future. To have a past or future, we must bring an interpretation
to some event which already is given in its primordial temporality. (Ph.P. p. 422: PP p. 483). In general Merleau-Ponty's view
departs from Husserl's notion of a central ego which constitutes
time through successive "protensions" and "retensions" since
he recognizes a primal acquisition of time out of which the
explicit temporal dimensions may be expressed.[18] He also
criticizes Heidegger's view of time as offered in *Being and Time*

which bases the present and past upon the future.[19] Again for Merleau-Ponty, the notion of the future depends upon an already acquired temporal field. How does this bear upon radical reflection? For Merleau-Ponty, the question is answered through considering different temporal relations. As we shall see, radical reflection and "the point where an individual begins to reflect upon himself" (Ph.P p. 62; PP p. 75) occurs as a presence of self to self which occurs when the background sense of time is brought into juxtaposition with the conceiving of time within some interpretation. His view here is difficult. As we shall see it finally calls again upon his notion of "foundation." It will be helpful to prepare a discussion of his understanding of radical reflection through a literary allusion, one which Merleau-Ponty himself supports on this issue.[20]

No work in French literature makes more of recollection and its virtues nor devotes more investigation to the topic of time than does Proust's *A Remembrance of Things Past*. Gary Madison in his commentary goes so far as to state of Proust's work "Proust accomplishes in the realm of literature what Merleau-Ponty attempts to do in philosophy."[21] How does Proust's work tell us anything about radical reflection? There are various analogies. Proust's novel ends with Marcel, modelled on Proust himself, discovering that he may recapture his past by writing a novel. The form of the novel would seem to be self-referring: a novel about writing a novel which is a novel about writing a novel, etc. But setting up such an infinite play of references misses that the story referred to and the planned acts of referring are quite different. Marcel depends for his recollection upon what Proust calls "involuntary memory." The novel that Marcel is ready to write will be organized, we presume, through the voluntary memory he presently has available to him. A difference lies between a past which is diffuse and disorganized but lived by his characters versus a past which is organized by the narrator and which is offered as an interpretation. This does not make for a self-referring structure, but a novel where one's experience of the past is brought into conjunction with an expression of the past. From the beginning of Proust's novel we are acquainted with the past as accessible and oddly co-present; it is "there" insofar as it is been preserved by the body.

> My body, the side upon which I was lying, loyally preserving from the past an impression which my mind should never have forgotten, brought back before my eyes the glimmering flame of the night-light in its bowl of Bohemian glass, shaped like an urn and hung by chains from the ceiling, and the chimney piece of Sienna marble in my bedroom at Combray, in my great-aunt's house, in those far-distant days which, at the moment of waking, seemed present without being clearly defined. (quoted in Ph.P. p. 181n.; PP p. 211n.)

Marcel's past re-enters his memory in such a way that the project of writing a novel does not amount to a self-referring enterprise. Proust instead offers us a making-present-of-the-past which allows us still to have the past as past while at the same time giving an interpretation of it. In fact Marcel's decision to write a novel straddles both the past which has come to him from involuntary memory with the project of making an interpretation of the past. There are, in fact, two features of Proust's novel which accord with Merleau-Ponty's account of radical reflection. First, both writers describe a confrontation with a past which is "there" but which is not reducible to express memories which we may contemplate, i. e. Proust's involuntary memory gives him access to this past. Merleau-Ponty refers to it as our "permanent acquisition" . . . "forever carried forward in time's succession." (Ph.P p. 393; PP p. 450–1) or "primordial temporality" (Ph.P p. 422; PP p. 483). Secondly, both writers maintain that the body, in its manner of involvement, regulates our accessibility to the past.

5. Eternity, "the atmosphere of time:" eternity and temporality are reciprocally founded

We have seen for Merleau-Ponty language and expression are founded in the body. This does not mean that any one particular human body produces or creates expression, but that the linguistic field and expression in general, come to be incorporated

116

into perceptual fields and into our natural and social worlds through the unity of the body-subject. Let us add to this that the interpenetration between language and the natural world is repeatedly set askew and new equilibria are struck through "authentic speech." Moreover the possibility of authentic speech creates a future which is related to what Merleau-Ponty calls "primordial time," "a past which has never been present."

> From these gains other acts of authentic expression—the writer's the artist's, or the philosopher's—are made possible. This ever-recreated opening in the plenitude of being is what conditions the child's first use of speech and the language of the writer, as it does the construction of the word and that of concepts. (Ph.P p. 197; PP p. 229)

Merleau-Ponty's use of "opening" (*ouverture*) in the passage above needs to be emphasized. In this case his view directly parallels Heidegger's notion of *Offenheit* as it is used in "The Origin of the Work of Art." Heidegger uses it to the same purpose in the following passage, for example:[22]

> . . . language alone brings what is, as something that is, into the Open for the first time. Where there is no language, as in the being of stone, plant and animal there is also no openness of what is, and consequently no openness either of that which is not and the empty.

How does authentic speech relate to temporality? In Merleau-Ponty's view the fact that authentic speech operates in "an opening within the plenitude of being" installs for us a future which is a breaking away from the "primordial time" of the natural world. The Italian musician, Luciano Berio has a *musique concrète* composition entitled *Visage* which consists in electronically produced noises—hisses, crashes and occasionally tones—that often approximate voice-like sounds. Mixed with the electronic music are non-verbal tone gestures which are sung by his wife. Often no sharp distinction can be drawn between the sounds of his wife and the electronic noise. Well into the *musique concrète* composition, the lulling, rumbling and crashing sounds are broken by the voice of his wife saying the word, *parole*. When she says this word, a shift occurs. We are ready for more of what she might say although we cannot imagine what it might be. The sounds heard before, at that point, are relegated to the background; now they appear meaningless. (Up to this point they were presumed to have musical significance.) What seems crucial is that once the non-verbal sounds are broken by the word, *parole*, we wait for the same opening to recur. The result is that this break henceforth prepares the possibility of a future to which we cannot in any away predict the outcome. Until the word, *parole*, the non-verbal sounds were bound by rhythms that filled our expectation of what was to come. With the word *parole*, a future which could truly be in excess of the past comes to be introduced.

In the quote above, Merleau-Ponty assigned authentic speech to three main locations: the writer's, the artist's, and the philosopher's. (Ph.P p. 197; PP pp. 229) In general they count as 1) the inauguration of authentic expression which depends on reference; 2) the inauguration of authentic expression which depends on non-referring expressions; and 3) the inauguration of authentic expression which stresses thought. If a novel, for example, determines a new configuration of characters or human events, it becomes itself testimony to the possibility of new constructions and configurations. It becomes a record which assures the possibility of a future which cannot be drawn, as yet, in accordance with the natural world. Merleau-Ponty often employs the somewhat difficult phrase that such acts of expression involve a "surplus of the signified over the signifying." (Ph.P. p. 390; PP p. 447) This phrase means that authentic expression surpasses the acquired significance it depends upon. The act of expression as such, "the signifying" falls short of the meanings that it suggests i. e. "the signified." A novelist completes his last work and finds that the work he has finished opens questions that require another book. There is more meaning in the work of the novel than the novelist intended in the act of writing of it. Hence, the expression, "the signified outruns the signifying." It is not a question of inadequacy of expression but that authentic expression is in principle directed towards a future which is "open" to the extent that its meaning cannot be wholly fixed by acquired significances already established. As such Proust's novel is symbolic of authentic expression since it ends with the opening of a possibility for expression: the novel ends with Marcel beginning to write.

The second case of authentic expression mentioned is the artist. Here it is a question of finding in mute phenomena new configurations which would also seem to make them "speak." ("Speak" is used here in the sense of authentic expression which has the main feature of "a surplus of the signified over the signifying.") We have already seen this exemplified in Merleau-Ponty's explication of Cezanne's work. As he says of Cezanne in *The Phenomenology*:

> Cezanne used to say of a portrait: 'If I paint in all the little blue and brown touches, I make him gaze as he does gaze . . . Never mind if they suspect how, by bringing together a green of various shades and a red, we sadden a mouth or bring a smile to a cheek.' (Ph.P p. 197; PP p. 230)

Cezanne discovers in patches of color how to create an expression which overruns their significance as bits of color. Furthermore, the successful engendering of expression by a collation of color marks a beginning. In a sense the developments of cubism and abstract expressionism are already implied in Cezanne's realistic figures. The creation of expression from bits of color opens another dimension to what might be offered by color.

We have seen how authentic expression opens a future which can not be drawn from our present or past. This allows for an installation of the beginning of a temporal flow. But as we have indicated, unlike Heidegger or Sartre, Merleau-Ponty holds that the temporal dimensions take place in relation to a permanent acquired past. As he states:

> To give expression is not to substitute, for new thought, a system of stable signs to which unchangeable thoughts are linked, it is to ensure, by the use of words already used, that the intention carries on the heritage of the past, it is at a stroke to incorporate the past into the present, and weld that present to a future, to open a whole temporal cycle in which the

"acquired" thought will remain present as a dimension, without our needing henceforth to summon up or reproduce it. (Ph.P. p. 392; PP p. 449–50)

In Merleau-Ponty's view, the expressions which we have acquired compose a field, which, as is the case with all fields for Merleau-Ponty at the time of *The Phenomenology*, observes a horizonal structure and includes indeterminate regions. This field is not just a collection of the *de facto* usages of a particular language. Just as the perceptual background can never be fully made into a figure; the whole of the linguistic field can never be made explicit. Some grounding of presumed meanings is required to allow for an expressive act to be meaningful. In Merleau-Ponty's view, the background of acquired expression, as a background, is permanently acquired. The result is that each act of expression which is drawn into the flow of time stands in relation to a background of expression which can never wholly be made present. Hence the permanence which occurs with any act of expression. It will *always* be true that the sentence I am now writing was written at some particular time, as it will *always* be true that the sentence that the reader is now reading was read at a particular time. It is no less true, in Merleau-Ponty's view, that time "flows." The passage of time is rooted in a sense of eternity. Eternity is not another order of time, but "the atmosphere of time". (Ph.P. p. 393; PP p. 451) Eternity and time also are another case of the interpenetration which the *Fundierung* relation expresses. Without a permanent acquisition an expression would not be grounded in a fixed set of significances; on the other hand without specific acts of expression the permanent acquisition of the linguistic background would not appear.

6. Radical reflection as self-reflecting authentic expression which is aware of its origins.

The core of philosophy is no longer an autonomous transcendental subjectivity, to be found everywhere and no where: it lies in the perpetual beginning of reflection, at the point where an individual life begins to reflect on itself. (Ph.P p. 62; PP p. 756)

Merleau-Ponty extends authentic expression to the writer, the artist and the philosopher. In the quote above he identifies the core of philosophy, *le centre de la philosophie*, at the perpetual beginning of reflection. We may now put together these various remarks and account for his notion of radical reflection and its relation to philosophy. Radical reflection involves three main aspects. First, radical reflection is a type of self-reflection and as such is an interrelationship of temporal fields. Second, radical reflection is a type of authentic expression and as such initiates a beginning or opening. Third, radical reflection may be distinguished among other kinds authentic expression insofar as it is aware of its origins. This distinguishes it as particularly authentic "philosophic" expression. Let us consider these three aspects.

In a passage in the chapter titled "Temporality," Merleau-Ponty sketches the overall framework which grounds self-reflection:

> We are saying that time *is* someone, or that temporal dimensions, insofar as they perpetually overlap, bear each other out and ever confine themselves to making explicit what was implied in each, being collectively expressive of that one single explosion or thrust which is subjectivity itself. (Ph.P p. 422; PP p. 482–3)

In Merleau-Ponty's view self-reflection occurs through a relation of the implicit to the explicit. In what Merleau-Ponty calls "primordial temporality," there is a set of relations that exists between parts of our field of experience which comes to be translated into explicit temporality. This precedent temporality, which is "a past which has never been a present," (Ph.P p. 242; PP p. 280) may be characterized according to regions which are accessible and near, and regions which are hidden and distant. (Here "near" and "distant" precede clear differentiation into the language of space and time. Regions of the field are pregnant with a sense of nearness or distance which is not yet organized according to the distinctions which follow when we ask the questions, Where? or When?) An apartment I see appears familiar and thereby "near" to me. The roots of a tree which are in front of the apartment are hidden and remote and are thereby distant and apart from me in this primitive sense of time. Further off is a street I am familiar with and thus is near since it more accessible to my actions. An alley which borders the street is hidden and thus according to my actions further away. In essence, in primordial temporality the field is given as a complex of relations that elicit temporality. Primordial temporality is implicit and does not deserve to be called "present" if it is compared to the temporality that occurs given expression. Given expression, we have the possibility of a genuine future, i.e. a future which is not equivalent to a recurring present or past moment. Furthermore as events take place in the opening which is allowed by a genuine future we have the arrival of a genuine present moment i. e. a fresh moment, a moment which cannot be identified with any other. Then as this present is eclipsed by a new present, we have an explicit past.

In Merleau-Ponty's view, what I have called implicit temporality already has sketched many of the relations which explicit temporality will define. The statement, "I will go home by way of Bond Street," initiates temporal relations which are already prepared by a world which prompts and elicits temporal distinctions. Now in Merleau-Ponty's view, the relation of implicit to explicit temporality allows for the possibility of self-reflection. We encounter the relationship of self to self as temporal in passages such as the following:

> It is the essence of time to be not only actual time, or time which flows, but also time which is aware of itself, for the explosion or dehiscence of the present towards a future is the archtype of the *relationship of self to self*, and it traces out an interiority or ipseity. (Ph.P. p. 426; PP p. 487)

As we shall see the term, "dehiscence," meaning a splitting or bursting out, is encountered often in Merleau-Ponty's later writings. He uses it repeatedly in *The Visible and the Invisible*. But at this point let us notice how we have a description of the notion of reflection in the phrase *relationship of self to self*. Self-reflection concerns sub-structures which make self-awareness possible. Through expression a social world bursts out, it becomes "hollowed out"—as Merleau-Ponty often says—from the natural world.[23] Expression allows for a "carrying on of the heritage of the past, it is at a stroke to incorporate the past into the present, and weld that present to a future, to open a whole temporal cycle in which the 'acquired' thought will remain present as a dimension, without our needing henceforth to summon it up or reproduce it." (Ph.P. p. 392; PP p. 450) The use of "dimension" in this quote should be stressed. In self-reflection, the explicit linguistic field becomes a dimension for the pre-linguistic. We are led along the wrong track if we imagine that it is a special act or method which we bring to our field of experience. In contrast to Husserl's view, self-reflection introduces no overviewing or observing subject. Reflection is not added to our world; it is rather a question of returning to one of its overlaps or fissures. Again the *Fundierung* relation is relevant. (Ph.P. p. 394; PP p. 351) The unreflected cannot be absorbed by the reflected because the reflected is determinate and explicit which the unreflected is not. On the other hand, the unreflected is not primary in the empiricist's sense because it is only through the reflected that it is made manifest.

The second feature of radical reflection is that the field of expression involves authentic expression. Radical reflection is a "perpetual beginning." We have already discussed how authentic expression makes possible a genuine future. Accordingly, radical reflection concerns an "originating event" wherein a genuine future for reflection is made possible. Confusion arises insofar as beginning is conceived here as a specific case of personal or historical origins. It is not a question of birthdates or the development of self-consciousness but the initiation of opportunity for reflection which remains permanently open. Consequently there is no question of a simple repose or agreement with oneself. Added to self-reflection, then, is an awareness of oneself which promises a genuine recommencement of reconsideration of one's condition.[24]

The third feature of radical reflection is awareness of its origins. Radical reflection is also an awareness of reflection.

Merleau-Ponty has associated radical reflection with what he takes to be requisite for evaluating philosophical discoveries. He states for example:

> Reflection cannot be thorough-going, or bring complete elucidation of its object, if it does not arrive at awareness of itself as well as its results . . . Only on this condition can philosophical knowledge become absolute knowledge . . . (Ph.P p. 62; PP p. 75)

Within a model wherein we add consciousness to ordinary awareness in the way that we put light to a page, we come to the view that reflecting on reflection requires that we also reflect on our last instance of reflection until we have a conceptual monster of the form that reflection consists in reflection on reflection on reflection . . . etc. But we have seen that reflection, for Merleau-Ponty, is not a faculty of attentiveness which is brought to bear on our experience; reflection is making explicit what is implicit in a the concrete richness of the world. The introduction of a supervening process or activity of reflection is unnecessary. What is relevant is the manner in which the reflected/unreflected juxtaposition is observed. Radical reflection is aware of itself as reflection just to the extent that it does not minimize the relation between the reflected and the unreflected. When Descartes determines in the Second Meditation that he is a thinking thing, he does not consider how traditions of certainty and Being are already shaping his conclusion. He is not aware that these issues have followed lines of thought that represent various detachments, false starts, and blind alleys preserved by a tradition which fails see that its reflections are founded in unreflected experience. The Cartesian *cogito* is perhaps only the most famous of reflections which hide their roots. Recurrent in Merleau-Ponty's thought is also Husserl's eidetic reduction which he insists can never take into account the whole of the world from which *eidos* is drawn. (cf. Ph.P pp. xvi-xvii. PP pp. xi-xii) The Cartesian and Husserlian discoveries are ingenious errors which minimize and eliminate the role of unreflected experience in the extreme. It is this elimination of the unreflected which would seem to be their strength but which in

124

Merleau-Ponty's view is precisely their error. Merleau-Ponty's radical reflection, on the contrary, insists on awareness of its origins in the unreflected. This does not imply the contradiction that the unreflected must become reflected. Rather, the inability to ever wholly bring the unreflected to explication be taken as a given. From this arises the consequences which further put radical reflection into perspective. First, given the irreducibility of unreflected experience radical reflection is certain of its incompleteness. Second, since radical reflection is incomplete we understand it to be certainly corrigible. Thirdly, and here Merleau-Ponty does make presumptions of the nature of unreflected experience, radical reflection is dependent upon unreflected experience which, although it cannot be brought to explicitation, is constant and unchanging. In accordance with this last point he states:

> . . . and finally that radical reflection amounts to a consciousness of its own dependence on an unreflective life which is its initial situation, unchanging, given once and for all. (Ph.P p. xiv; PP p. ix)

In summary then, radical reflection is an awareness of self made possible by the reciprocal foundation of the reflected on the unreflected wherein a manner of authentic expression creates a beginning which cannot wholly be made into a past event and which is aware of itself as reflection which is incomplete, corrigible yet dependent upon an unchanging unreflected world.

In passing let us note that we may draw a parallel between Merleau-Ponty and Heidegger in regards to radical reflection. For Heidegger, thought, as discussed for example in the "Letter on Humanism," is shown to be stripped from its true nature by being conceived as logic. "Logic" derives from "logos" which in turn even more radically may be derived from "legein," to gather, to harvest, to collect. Thinking is to re-collect Being and to bring it to disclosure through the *Lichtung*. The reflected stands to the unreflected in radical reflection similarly to the way that *denken* stands to Being. Levels of falling away from radical reflection can be established in Merleau-Ponty's account. Introspection and what he calls "analytic reflection" (cf. Ph.P pp.

226, 238; PP pp. 261, 275) are various manners in which the reflected is separated off from the unreflected. In introspection mental phenomena are severed from their directedness towards a world. In analytic reflection, our primary encounter with a world of things is withheld in favor of breaking up perception into qualities and sensations. Similarly for Heidegger, thinking would leave off its origins and make logical rules and principles into the source by which we describe and determine thought. Thinking finally descends to calculative reckoning and becomes in a word "thoughtless." If mythology can help to suggest an overview of the detachment that reflection and thinking are prey to, we can say that, like Cronos who dethrones his parents, Uranus and Gaea, heaven and earth, reflection and thinking sever themselves from their origins in the unreflected and Being. But there are also differences between Merleau-Ponty's and Heidegger's views. First, Heidegger's *denken* is successful to the extent that it recollects Being. The very fact that Heidegger relates thinking to Being secures his views in terms of one main consideration i. e. questioning "what is." Merleau-Ponty on the other hand, leads us to suppose that questions relating to the nature of the mind are fundamentally important. After all, it is the mind or consciousness which reflects. Secondly, for Heidegger, thinking is successful to the extent that it brings us into the nearness of Being. Being itself is never delineated. The unreflected for Merleau-Ponty on the other hand is a more fixed notion. It is assumed to be the grounding of the natural world out of which our pact with the natural world emerges. Language, reflection and thought are in turn founded in it and *vice versa*. In short, the unreflected for Merleau-Ponty is the unreflected of the natural world. Heidegger makes no such distinction between a natural and social world.

Notes To Chapter Three

[1] Husserl, *Logical Investigations*, Volume Two, Findlay translation, Routledge & Kegan Paul, London, 1970, p. 463.

[2] Ibid, p. 477.

[3] Husserl, *Formal and Transcendental Logic*, translated by Dorion Cairns, The Hague, Martinus Nijhoff, 1969, pp. 78–79.

126

4 Husserl. *Logical Investigations*, op. cit., p. 475.

5 Plato has Socrates say in the *Cratylus*, Stephanus page number 425d, for example:

> Socrates: That objects should be imitated in letters and syllables, and so find expression, may appear ridiculous, Hermogenes, but it cannot be avoided—there is no better principle to which we can look for the truth of first names.

Plato, *The Dialogues of Plato*, Jowett translation, Random House, New York, 1937, Vol. I, p. 214

6 Darwin, *The Expression of the Emotions*, p. 34

7 Paget, Sir Richard, *Human Speech*, Routledge & Kegan Paul Ltd, London, reprinted in 1963, p. 133.

8 See for example Ph.P p. 394.

9 Mallin, Samuel B., *Merleau-Ponty's Philosophy*, Yale University Press, New York, 1979.

Although Mallin finds in the notion of sublimation an appropriateness which leads him to see both the usage found in psychoanalysis as well as the usage found in chemistry as relevant. He states: "Merleau-Ponty uses this term so as to allow connotations from its use both in psychoanalysis and chemistry." (Ibid, p. 169) He later stresses that "Sublimation is only one side of a process which reverses itself by making the founded structures influence the preflective situations that ground them." (Ibid. p. 197) Mallin appreciates that the foundation that exists between language and the perceptual world is not unilateral. But his presentation, by stressing sublimation, returns us to the causal mode of thinking as did Freud's use of sublimation. Both lead us to wonder how the expansiveness of linguistic cultural acquisition could ever hope to find full correlation to bodily gesture, just as Freud's account of da Vinci's undeveloped psychosexuality fails to offer a sufficiently broad account for the extraordinary variety of his creative work.

10 See Silverman's forward to *Consciousness and the Acquisition of Language*, notes drawn from Merleau-Ponty's lectures given at the Sorbonne 1949–51, p. xiii.

11 For a fuller account of Merleau-Ponty's understanding of Saussure's theory of signs as diacritical see "Indirect Language and the Voices of Silence" as reprinted in *Signs*, translated by McCleary, Northwestern University Press, 1964, pp. 39–40.

12 Merleau-Ponty, *Consciousness and the Acquisition of Language*, translated by Hugh Silverman, Northwestern University Press, Evanston, 1973, p. 90.

13 Heidegger. *On the Way to Language*, translated by Peter D. Hertz, Harper and Row, New York, 1971, p. 111.

14 op. cit. in "A Dialogue on Language between a Japanese and an Inquirer," p. 53.

15 See also Ph.P. p. 220; PP p. 255; for remarks on radical reflection.

16 Ballard, Edward G., "On Cognition of the Pre-Cognitive—Merleau-Ponty," *Philosophical Quarterly*, 11:44 (July, 1961), pp. 238–44.

17 de Waelhens, Alphonse, *Une Philosophie de l'ambiguité: L'Existentialisme de Maurice Merleau-Ponty*, Publications Universitaire de Louvain, 1951, Louvain, pp. 399–400, my translation.

18 In passages such as the following, Merleau-Ponty criticizes Husserl's approach which allocates structuring of time a constituting ego:

They [the present, past and future] do not run from a central *I*, but from my perceptual field itself, so to speak, which draws along in its wake its own horizon of retentions, and bites into the future with its protensions. I do not pass through a series of instances of now, the images of which I preserve and which, placed end to end make a line. (Ph.P. p. 416; PP p. 476)

[19] See Ph.P p. 427; PP p. 489; for Merleau-Ponty's criticism of Heidegger views on temporality.

[20] Consider for example: "We are, as Proust declared, perched upon a pyramid of past life, and if we do not see this, it is because we are obsessed by objective thought. We believe that our past, for ourselves, is reducible to the express memories which we are able to contemplate." (Ph.P p. 393; PP p. 450)

[21] Madison, Gary, *The Phenomenology of Merleau-Ponty*, Ohio University Press, Athens Ohio, 1981, p. 135

[22] Albert Hofstadter's translation at it appears in *Poetry, Language and Thought*, Harper & Row, New York, 1971, p. 72.

[23] In his Eighth Duino Elegy, Rilke describes a taking leave which is elemental to our lives. Rilke's poem depends upon the notion that human nature is split away from itself. This compares to Merleau-Ponty's view which sees self-reflection as grounded in a fundamental separation of self with self. Rilke emphasizes taking leave. From Merleau-Ponty's point of view this is one form that the separation may take. One may also find in it the markings of a beginning. Consider the following lines from the Eighth Elegy:

> Who's turned us round like this, so that we always,
> do what we may, retain the attitude
> of someone who's departing? Just as he,
> on the last hill, that shows him all his valley
> for the last time, will turn and stop and linger,
> we live our lives, for ever taking leave.

> Wer hat uns also umgredeht, dass wir,
> was wir auch tun, in jener Haltung sind
> von einem, welcher forgeht? Wie er auf
> dem letzten Hügel, der ihm ganz sein Tal
> noch einmal zeigt, sich wendet, anhält, weilt—
> so leben wir und nehmen immer Abschied.
>   Rilke, *Duino Elegies*, Die Achte Elegie, 70–5.

Rilke, Rainer Maria, *Duino Elegies*, translation by Leishman and Spender, W. W. Norton Company, New York, 1963.

[24] This moment of presence of self to self through a turning back in expression is retained in Merleau-Ponty's later writings. Merleau-Ponty maintains the same view in *Signs* for example and calls it the human movement *par excellence*. As he states:

> To explain the *Mona Lisa* by the sexual history of Leonardo da Vinci or to explain it by some divine motion Leonardo was the instrument of or by some human nature capable of beauty still involves giving way to the retrospective illusion, realizing the valuable in advance—misunderstanding the human movement *par excellence* in which a life woven out of chance events turns back upon, regrasps, and expresses itself. (*Signs* p. 240, S. p. 305)

4

Flesh composed of suns—
"How can such be?" exclaim the simple ones.
Robert Browning, *Parleyings with Certain People*[1]

The *Visible and the Invisible* and the Discovery of the Chiasm

We see that hand pointing to us in *The Nightwatch* is truly there only when we see that its shadow on the captain's body presents it simultaneously in profile. The spatiality of the captain lies at the meeting place of two lines of sight which are incompossible and yet together. Everyone with eyes has at some time or other witnessed this play of shadows, or something like it, and has been made by it to see a space and the things included therein. But it works in us without us; it hides itself in making the object visible. (EM p. 167)

The Nightwatch did not acquire its title until the late 18th Century. The formal title first given to the work was the more magisterial "The Company of Captain Frans Banning Cocq and Lieutenant Willem van Ruytenburch." The two individuals mentioned in the title are prominently displayed in the center of the canvass. The captain is adorned in the black uniform on the left; the lieutenant in the brilliantly yellow uniform on the right. Its title "The Nightwatch" is in fact inappropriate on two counts. First, Rembrandt did not paint a nighttime scene. The darkness attributed to the painting was largely the result of layers of dirt and varnish applied to the painting over centuries. Secondly, Rembrandt did not paint a watch. By the time this painting was made, the daily keeping of a watch was already an anachronism. Rembrandt's intentions were more ambitious. To the eighteen militiamen who were depicted in the painting—

mostly wealthy wholesale dealers—Rembrandt added sixteen other figures who were not part of actual citizenry. The additional figures were dressed in costumes from different periods. Through their actions and equipment Rembrandt wove allegorical and historical allusions into the scene. He portayed customs which were part of the times of the painting, but he also implied the historical traditions of the city. As E. Haverkamp-Begemann indicates in his recent study, Rembrandt represented in this painting the preparedness and readiness of Amsterdam's citizenry to fight for Amsterdam's rights. "For their contemporaries, this group portrait of eighteen men undoubtedly signified a glorification of Amsterdam, the most successful and powerful city of its time."[2]

In the quote from the "Eye and the Mind" that heads this chapter, Merleau-Ponty refers to a feature of this masterpiece which often goes unnoticed. "We see that hand pointing to us in *The Nightwatch* is *truly there* [my emphasis] only when we see that its shadow on the captain's body presents it simultaneously in profile." The extended hand of the captain is central to the composition of the painting and conveys a remarkable sense of both openness and reserved strength. But there is an enigma in its shadow. The shadow cast by the captain's hand on the lieutenant's coat suggests that the sun is approximately 45 degrees to the left of the captain. (The shadow is prominently visible, since in at least the restored version of the painting—not a nightwatch but a "daywatch"—the lieutenant's uniform is brilliantly illuminated.) The shadow cast from the captain's extended foot, however, implies an altogether different angle. Through these "illogical" shadows we are given at once an open hand—as in profile—while as the same time we are given a hand which hidden and reserved. Both of these points of view are, as Merleau-Ponty says, "incompossible." They are not views which we can have at once. Such a play of shadows could not be recorded by a photograph. Now, from Merleau-Ponty's point of view, this painting gives us the "being of the extended hand" which a simple photograph could not capture. It is not a question of the trompe l'oeil which Rembrandt made use of nor even of his extraordinary mastery of illumination which has led one critic to refer to him as "his own sun-god."[3] In Merleau-Ponty's view Rembrandt's use of shadows and illumination reveal an understanding of the conditions of presence and Being. The hand is "truly there" because of the incompossibility of views. This painting in fact can be taken as paradigmatic of a main thesis that we will discuss as it occurs in his last work, *The Visible and the Invisible*. An "encroachment" of incompossible views is a requirement of any being just because it is by such an incompossiblity that an opening or space is engendered wherein new perspectives, open-endedly, may be discovered. In other words beings, insofar, as they are given as "there" require incompossibility. Let us make this main thesis of Merleau-Ponty's later work clear.

In the discussion of *The Phenomenology* we saw that the body-subject operates in a "pact" with the natural world and so establishes the lived world of perception. Cognitive and linguistic fields "interpenetrate" and are reciprocally founded in the perceptual world. In his later works however—already in "The Eye and the Mind" for example—Merleau-Ponty introduces a different approach to the issue of interpenetration of fields. In his later work, instead of seeing the body-proper/perceptual world and its interworking with cognitive and linguistic fields as a system which comprises our world, he comes to view the "doubling up" (*dédoublement*) (VI p. p. 139; *VI* p. 183) of one field upon another as the manner by which we "belong to" Being. He states in a Working Note: "Each field is a dimensionality, and Being is dimensionality itself." (VI p. 227; *VI* p. 280) He implies here that a lack of successful integration of fields is a requirement of Being. In Merleau-Ponty's last works he moves from an orientation which sees us rooted in a world through our pact with the natural world, that is from an existentialism and a version of being-in-the-world (*l'être au monde*), to an "indirect" ontology (cf. VI p. 179; *VI* p. 233) wherein it is claimed that the various fields we establish indicate ways in which we are possessed or belong to Being (*l'être en est*). (VI pp. 100, 123, 127, 261; pp. *VI* 136, 164, 169, 314).

The difficulties in expressing his later views are extensive. They arise when we attempt to describe our relation to Being in a manner which does not reify the notion. For Merleau-Ponty, Being is evidenced by a "separation" (*écart*) of fields (VI pp. 7, 124, 148, 171, 194–97; *VI* pp. 23, 166, 194, 245, 248–51). The terms he employs to describe this separation vary. He refers to a "cleavage" (*clivage*) (VI p. 214; *VI* p. 268), a "dehiscence" (*dehiscence*) (VI pp. 117, 263; *VI* pp. 157, 316) or a "hiatus" (VI p. 148; *VI* p. 195). And the language used to describe the overlapping of fields is similarly varied. He describes an "encroachment" (*empiétement*) (VI p. 134; *VI* p. 177), a "criss-crossing" (*recroisement*) (VI p. 133; *VI* p. 176), a "coiling up" (*enroulement*) (VI p. 114; *VI* p. 153), "a redoubling" (*redoublement*) (VI p. 114; *VI* p. 153). On occasion he uses language which suggests mysticism. He describes his indirect ontology as a return to the *Sige*, to the abyss. (VI p. 179; *VI* p. 233). Insofar as a mystical approach implies some direct access to Being or the One which few individuals attain, however, his view is not mystical. He uses the term "abyss" to suggest that Being cannot be directly encountered. His notion of an "indirect ontology" is apt insofar as he holds that Being is evinced just because it is indirectly confronted as that which allows for an overlapping of fields. Being may be inquired into as a "support" which comes into the world—a "negativity which comes into the world" (VI p. 250; *VI* p. 303). As he admits, his later philosophy which he calls a "negative philosophy" can be likened to "negative theology" by which we are to understand an approach to God or gods which would set up an inquiry by affirming what God or gods are not. (VI p. 179; *VI* p. 233) Comparisons like this one fail, however, if the analogy is followed too closely. Being, in principle, for Merleau-Ponty is neither specifically theological nor mundane. It cannot be encapsulized by an ontology which would offer an account or description of it. The concatenation of fields is never wholly accomplished. This is a positive phenomenon, which until proven otherwise, presages the possibility of the overlapping of other fields. Being is intimated by the cleavage or separation of fields.

1. The fundamental pattern which adumbrates Being: the chiasm

In spite of the fact that *The Visible and Invisible* is Merleau-Ponty's last work, which he was writing at the time of his death and which he left unfinished, it has the tone of a beginning. This is partly due to the fact that Merleau-Ponty invents a new idiom for treating an array of classical dichotomies which include mind/body, essence/existence, and subject/object relations. His introduction of the "chiasm" and "flesh" as well as the special sense he gives to the "visible" and the "invisible" reflect his project of forging new expressions. It is important to see even from the beginning that the introduction of these new terms does not only include an offering of a new set of philosophic distinctions. Merleau-Ponty, in all likelihood, held that a new way of speaking about philosophical problems needed to be invented. Traditional terminology is ensconced with confusions to the extent that to pose questions in traditional concepts is to invite former impasses. The scope of the reformation of conceptual apparatus he has in mind can be discerned from passages such as the following:

> Replace the notions of concepts, idea, mind, representation with the notions of *dimensions*, articulations, level, hinges, pivots, configurations—(VI p. 224; *VI* p. 277)

As we shall see dimensions, articulations, levels, hinges, pivots and configurations are different ways of referring to aspects of Being as universal dimensionality. The chiasm is a crossing over of fields which allows for "hinges" and "pivots." And, the relation of the "visible" to the "invisible" involves a fresh understanding of configuration. Within a philosophy which proposes elemental conceptual revisions, terms such as "flesh" or "the chiasm" which are anomalous to the language of traditional philosophy are desirable: they prevent the reader from orienting himself within traditional lines of thought.

Among these new terms, of primary importance is Merleau-Ponty's notion of the chiasm. First, we may note that the term "chiasm" occurs ordinarily in two contexts: In anatomy, the crossing of the optic nerves on the ventral surface of the brain is called the optic chiasm. And, in rhetoric, a reversal of parallel phrases or clauses in the second line of a two line couplet is also called a chiasm or "chiasmus." Merleau-Ponty is drawing upon the first usage in devising a notion which will describe a paradigmatic manner in which fields interrelate. As he states:

> . . . like the chiasm of the eyes, this one is also what makes us belong to the same world—a world which is not projective, but forms its unity across incompossibilities such as that of *my* world and the world of the other . . . (VI p. 215; *VI* p. 268)

A simple version of the chiasm relation appears in the "reversibility" of touch. Merleau-Ponty notes the reversibility of the touch on several occasions beginning with *The Phenomenology* wherein he states that this feature of the body is "sufficient to distinguish it from objects." (Ph.P. p. 93; PP p. 109) There his observations, in turn, are derived from Husserl who describes on several occasions a "kind of reflection" which takes place as the left hand touches the right.[4] In his later writings Merleau-Ponty greatly develops this reversibility.

The phenomenon is simple enough. The touching hand may be thought of as a kind of probing missile, "an exploratory power" (*Signs*, p. 166) and the hand touched, a living bundle of skin, muscle and bone which may be felt. When the touching hand stops actively probing, a reversal or "reflection" takes place. The touching hand "takes its place among the things it touches." It is "in a sense one of them [and] opens finally upon a tangible being of which it is also a part." (VI p. 133; *VI* p. 176). This experience which usually goes unnoticed is a simple instance of the chiasm relation. The "reflection of the body" as it shifts from touching to taking its place among the things it touches is an example of an overlapping of fields wherein there is a "non-difference" (VI p. 255; *VI* p. 309) between fields. Merleau-

Ponty's point is that the overlapping of fields involves just enough reflection to allow one field to belong to another. But the reversal is never complete. One field is not circumscribed by another. If I could make my touching body, when touching, wholly into an object that might be touched, I would be able to map one field wholly onto another. In this case the field of touch and of being touched would wholly overlap. But they do not do so. There is instead "a reciprocal insertion and intertwining of one in the other." (VI. p. 138; *VI* p. 182) This "reciprocal insertion" as opposed to a coextensive mapping of one field onto another allows for the existence of a "sensible Being." We should recall here that for Merleau-Ponty, Being is adumbrated by fields which co-exist, overlap, but maintain a separation (*écart*) or cleavage. It is just the lack of fully realized reversibility in the touch which gives ontological proportions to the tangibility of the body. As he states:

> The touching of oneself and the touch have to be understood as each the reverse of each other—The negativity that inhabits the touch (and which I must not minimize: it is because of it that the body is not an empirical fact, that it has ontological signification) . . . (VI p. 255; *VI* p. 308)

A second experience which reflects the chiasm relation occurs in vision. Seeing, Merleau-Ponty states, as a palpitation of the eye is only a "remarkable variant" of tactile palpitation (VI p. 133; *VI* p. 175). If we consider looking at a cup on a table, we find that there are exploratory movements and also a fixing of the table with the gaze. But these two phases of perception need to be complemented by a third. After the gaze has lighted upon an object, one senses oneself as potentially a visible thing. Vision involves the same reversal as touch. Again we are never so visible as the objects that we see. Rather our vision opens us to the possibility of being seen, but this possibility is never the same as our seeing another. It "is imminent and never realized in fact." (VI. p. 147; *VI* p. 194) "I will never see my own retinas, but if one thing is certain for me it is that *one* would find at the bottom of my eyeballs those dull and secret membranes." (VI.

135

p. 146; *VI* p. 192) Again, as in the case of touch, from Merleau-Ponty's point of view, the implication of my visibility without its full realization by me is responsible for the manner in which I am "a visible being." Merleau-Ponty finds in the relation of seer to seen, and toucher to touched, a pattern which illuminates the requirements for there to be a seeing or touching *being*.

> There is vision, touch, when a certain visible, a certain tangible, turns back upon the whole of the tangible, of which it is a part, or when suddenly it finds itself *surrounded* by them, or when between it and them, and through their commerce, is formed a Visibility, a Tangibility in itself, which belong properly neither to the body qua fact nor to the world qua fact—as upon two mirrors facing one another where two indefinite series of images set in one another arise which belong really to neither of the two surfaces, since each is only the rejoinder of the other, and which therefore form a couple, a couple more real than either of them. (VI p. 139; *VI* p. 183)

The last sentence of this quote is particularly directed to the issue of the encroachment of fields. The entering of the seer into the world of things seen—this turning back—forms, as he states, a couple "more real than either of them." The metaphor is apt. Mirrors facing each other create innumerable pairs of fronts and backs. But it is the incompossible encroachment of these paired views that allows for the existence of an individual. The encroachment indicates an individual "more real" than a simple overlaying of views.

The chiasm relation, of which we have considered two elemental cases, is in Merleau-Ponty's later works a fundamental patterning which adumbrates any particular being. As a result he is highly interested in describing types of this "fundamental fission or segregation." As we shall see this line of thinking gives him a new approach to dualities as broad as mind and body or subject and object.

Let us continue to explore basic versions of the chiasm relation. There is a chiasm relation between touch and vision.

It is a marvel too little noticed that every movement of my eyes—even more every displacement of my body—has its place in the same visible universe that I itemize and explore with them, as conversely, every vision takes place somewhere in tactile space. (VI. p. 134; *VI* p. 177)

In describing the chiasm that exists between touch and vision, Merleau-Ponty is rethinking his view in *The Phenomenology*. There, an object was intersensorial inasmuch as the body-subject was alerted as a whole to act upon it. This cup of coffee I see is given with tactile, gustatory and olfactory aspects. This is because my body in its readiness to perform an action functions as a synergistic system and finds in the cup the pole of the directedness of my bodily actions. But we must add to this view that a mapping of the visible world, as a whole, onto the tangible world, as a whole, is prepared in advance by the reversal of the body. As the body at one phase of the act of seeing takes its place among the visible, so the body as an intersensorial perceiver takes its place in a world that in principle leads us to suppose a blending of multi-sensorial aspects. Given the reversibility of the body we are left to find how objects in the world are multi-sensorial.

The chiasm relation also appears in our sense of the movement of our bodies. There is a blend of moving ourselves and being moved in ordinary action.

I say of a thing that it is moved; but my body moves itself, my movement deploys itself. It is not ignorant of itself; it is not blind for itself; it radiates from a self . . . (EM p. 162)

Objects in the world are moved. The cup is moved to another table. We also can be moved, but this amounts to a limiting case of our divesting ourselves of our motility—an extension of a possibility which is realized only momentarily for us. Even if we are tied or bound we shortly return to centering ourselves in a setting and make ourselves a center for moving objects. As Merleau-Ponty states, in ordinary immediate experience we take ourselves to be "a zero of movement even during movement." (VI p. 255; *VI* p. 308) The question arises as to the manner in which we conceive ourselves as "self-moving". Again the reversibility suggested by the chiasm relation describes the degree to which we "objectify." We never move ourselves as we move an object even though there is "an imminence" to our being moved as an object. (VI. p. 249; *VI* p. 303) And again, the reversibility is suggested in principle but it is never fully accomplished. Just as I take my place among visible things because I see, I also take my place among movable objects by moving things. This is enough to establish that I am a "self-moving" being. As in the other cases, the apprehension of oneself as self-moving requires that there are two maps, in this case a map of motility and a second of the perceptual world, which are complete yet not superposable.

A chiasm relation also exists between speaking and listening. I can in principle listen to my own speech but it is not "objectified" any more than my touching or seeing is. My listening allows me to take a place among a world of speakers. And again it is the reversibility of the phenomenon which establishes a kind of being. In this case it establishes what he calls "the named I," (*Le Je denommé*). (VI p. 246; *VI* p. 299) As in all cases of reversibility the being which is established is taken to be a manner of separation which permits open-enddedly additional interpretations, yet is in itself ungraspable.

> The speaking-listening duality remains at the heart of the I, its negativity is but the *hollow* between speaking and hearing, the point where there equivalence is formed. (VI p. 246; *VI* p. 300)

The last version of the chiasma relation we will discuss concerns the insertion or inscription of language into the natural world.

> In a sense, if we were to make completely explicit the architectonics of the human body, its ontological framework, and how it sees itself and hears itself, we would see that the structure of its mute world is such that all the possibilities of language are already given in it. Already our existence as seers (that is, we said as beings who turn the world back upon itself . . . and especially our existence as sonorous beings for

others and for ourselves contain everything required for there to be speech from the one to the other, speech about the world. (VI. p. 155; *VI* p. 203)

Merleau-Ponty indicates here the remarkable extension he is giving to the chiasm relation. The whole of the interworkings of natural and social worlds are finally understood to involve the intertwining of the chiasm relation. In the quote above he accounts for the genesis of the namable and the sayable out of a mute world. The silence out of which speech is formed is prepared by the reversibility of the body. "As there is a reflexivity of the touch, of sight, and the touch-vision system, there is a reflexivity of the movements of phonation and hearing; they have their sonorous inscription, the vociferations have in me their motor echo." (VI. p. 144; *VI* p. 190) Because of the reversibility of the body which extends across touch, vision, and phonation, the babbling of a child prepares a listening of the mute world. At the moment that the child's babbling is coupled over with its own listening, it becomes a speaking being. As in all cases of reversibility, the child henceforth allows himself to take a place in a world that can be listened to; the world henceforth is given as a bedrock for effability. The world is no longer mute but in principle crossed over with a silence which presages or promises the possibility of speech. ". . . there is initiation, that is not the positing of a content, but the opening of a dimension that can never be closed again . . ." (VI p. 151; *VI* p. 198) There is no question of the "destruction or conservation of silence" (VI p. 154; *VI* p. 202) anymore than there is a question of the destruction of the tangibility or visibility of the world. (In many ways Merleau-Ponty's theory of the chiasma presages the discoveries of Heinz Kohut. Kohut's theory of the self takes as fundamental that the development of the self demands the mirroring of a child by an empathetic parent or parental figure.)[5]

The initial essay in *Signs*, "Indirect Language and the Voices of Silence," suggests the relation of language to a mute world even in its title. "All language is indirect or allusive—that is if you wish, silence." (*Signs* p. 43). This statement, as much as any in the essay, expresses the recurrent thought of the essay. Merleau-Ponty introduces the notion of silence into Saussure's diacritical theory of language. (As mentioned in an earlier chapter Merleau-Ponty incorporated Saussure's diacritical theory of meaning into his own work on expression as early as 1947.) For Saussure, let us recall, the meaning of a term is determined by the *difference* that that term marks from other terms. Language is *indirect* because it operates by allusion to other terms. When a new expression is coined, its difference which is yet to be formulated opens upon an "unvoiced difference." No word has yet appeared. It appears as a difference open to a silence from which the new term might be voiced. We come then to the sense of Merleau-Ponty's saying that language is "indirect" and opens upon a "inventive" silence. (VI p. 268; *VI* p. 322) Let us make more explicit the role of silence in its relation to speech. 1) The meaning of terms is established by the difference between terms. 2) Acquired meanings are established expressions which first were cases of authentic speech. (He maintains in his later works, as he did in *The Phenomenology* that "Empirical language can only be the result of creative language.") (*Signs* p. 44) 3) Authentic speech arises from an "inventive" silence that is in relation to a difference which is in the process of becoming fixed but which begins with no decided connection to voiced speech. This rooting of speech in an originating or formulative silence completes a survey of the basic architecture of the chiasma relation.

Let us summarize what we have found so far regarding Merleau-Ponty's theory of the chiasma. The chiasm relation is paradigmatic of our indirect relation to Being. It describes a multitude of human/world relations. Fundamental instances of the chiasma relation involve the nexus of seer to seen, toucher to touched, vision to touch, movement to fixed objects, speech to listening and finally, by a further crossing over of the visual-tactile world with speech and listening, the nexus of the silent world to expression. Being is adumbrated as the hiatus, separation, or dehiscence of the sides of the chiasm relation. The net result is a world linked through a webbing of "non-different" sides. Not properly thought of as a unity, which would make it into one thing, nor a synthesis which would bring it under one concept, but a "unicity" (unicité) (VI pp. 228, 233; *VI* pp. 282, 286) a term Merleau-Ponty introduces which like "facticity" implies an awareness of the errors of objective thought. In the case of "unicity," the revision over unity entails that unification is achieved provisionally, within adjustments to a network of chiasm relations, always subject to reformulation, and acquiring new adumbrations of Being, which is given as supportive of the separation of the chiasm.

2. The chiasm as an ontological element: the flesh

Merleau-Ponty's notion of "flesh" is based in a transformed conception of level or norm. The notion of a level first arose in *The Phenomenology of Perception* in regard to perceptual constancies. Optimal distance, illumination, and verticality required the establishment of levels through which the body-subject attains a maximum of richness and clarity. In his last writings, levels, norms, axes and dimensions are employed to account for field phenomena in a new way. Before the language of levels and norms had been employed to distinguish a "neutral" or a "point-zero" within a field. The field was taken to be a positive phenomenon which was organized by a level. His later treatment of levels indicates a shift inasmuch as he makes the Saussurian notion of *meaning as difference* so elemental to his thinking that levels become an index of a coherent difference. In other words, instead of thinking of levels as a way of adjusting an orientation within a field, in his later thought, there is no field apart from its relation to levels as a difference from that level. Many expressions reflect this revision; for example, he discusses an "index of the coherent deformation" (*Signs* p. 54, 81) "deviation in a system of equivalences" (*Signs* p. 61), a "never-finished differentiation" (VI p. 153; *VI* p. 201), or the "integral of all the differentiations" (VI p. 155; *VI* p. 203).

Let us put aside ways in which we are mislead in our effort to understand Merleau-Ponty's notion of "flesh." First, there is a problem in translating the French *chair*. It is granted that the term is unconventional as a philosophical term in both French and English and Merleau-Ponty intends to break with traditional thought by such an unconventional usage. We should also note, however, that the English term brings with it a carnality which the French word does not. Other candidates for translation, such as "bodiliness" or "corporality" miss the sense of the French term even more. These two possibilities suggest abstractions when Merleau-Ponty clearly seeks something concrete and tangible—an "element" as he states. Merleau-Ponty's notion can be more closely understood if one keeps with the French usage and stresses features of pliability, aliveness and softness. Those aspects associated with carnage should be deemphasized.

Secondly, Merleau-Ponty tells us he considers the flesh to be a "*general thing*, midway between the spatio-temporal individual and the thing . . . an 'element' of Being." (VI p. 139; *VI* p. 184) Confusions can easily follow from this line of discussion if we think that he is doing old style metaphysics and the flesh is a concept of Being. Merleau-Ponty states in a Working Note, "*One cannot make a direct ontology.*" (VI p. 179; *VI* p. 233) Being is not a circumscribable concept. Merleau-Ponty tells us instead that the flesh is an element in the sense of the "old term . . . that was used to speak of water, air, earth, and fire." (VI p. 139; *VI* p. 184) The sense of the old term, Merleau-Ponty has in mind, is likely the same that is employed by Aristotle, for example in *Metaphysics*, Z, 17. Aristotle speaks of material, mathematical, and linguistic elements. Aristotle's usage reflects a notion of elements as fundamental *styles* of being. Similarly, the flesh is a style of Being. The flesh is not matter, mind, nor substance but "a sort of incarnate principle that brings a style of being wherever there is a fragment of being." (VI p. 139; *VI* p. 184)

How does the notion of flesh relate to Merleau-Ponty's later discussions of level or dimensions? In a description of a woman passing by Merleau-Ponty indicates his usage of "flesh."

142

A woman passing by is not first and foremost a corporeal contour for me, a colored mannequin, or a spectacle; she is an "an individual, sentimental, sexual expression." She is a certain manner of being flesh which is given entirely in her walk or even in the shock of her heel on the ground—as the tension of a bow in present in each fiber of the wood—a very noticeable variation in the norm of walking, looking touching and speaking that I possess in my self-awareness because I am incarnate. (*Signs* p. 54)

In this quote the language of levels, dimensions and coherent deformations is elemental. The style of the woman's walk and even the shock of her heel are levels or dimensions in the sense that they mark a variation in her other movements. Merleau-Ponty finds in this relation a secret to the style of this woman's manner of being. The shock of the woman's heel is an index which gives sense to her posture and gestures because of the way that the shock of a heel integrates other aspects of her behavior as differences from it. The sound of the woman's heel on pavement makes sense of a less assertive, flexible bodily stance. It attunes us to the sensibility, let us say, that the woman has adopted the manner of being bold and decisive in the public world. If we catch sight of her face and it reveals an easy and responsive expression we understand this expression according to the marked rhythm of her walk. By a bit of behavior, we are given access to the woman's attitude and to her overall style of involvement. For Merleau-Ponty, the sound of the heel on the pavement is not a perception among other perceptions. Rather it is a neutral which gives us access to an overall attitude. The language of levels and norms as paired with "coherent deviations" is fundamental. These concepts allows us to rethink how the woman's involvement is *in* the behavior that we see. In fact to understand how a level may be in a field of differences a new notion of "in" needs to be distinguished. We may distinguish, first, the "in" of containment as in "the cup is *in* the cupboard." Secondly, we may distinguish the "in" of involvement. The "in" of involvement figures into expressions such as he is *in* business or he is *in* doubt. (Within the existential tradition, the "in" of involvement appears paradigmatically in the expression "being-in-the-world.") Now we need to distinguish a third sense of "in." Here we have an "in" which marks an index of systematic difference. Merleau-Ponty often indicates that manner of "in" as "non-difference." (cf. VI p. 225; *VI* p. 309) But it occurs most regularly in the expression "in-visible" through which he describes "invisibles" which are in the visible as indexes of systematic difference.

Merleau-Ponty, in reappraising issues in the history of art in his two late essays "The Eye and the Mind" and "Indirect Language and the Voices of Silence," describes how an "in-visible" is built into the visible world. He refers to the "innocence" of painting. (See EM p. 161) The painter is innocent because he is least capable of hiding his innovations. Unlike music, drama or literature, painting is readily linked to the natural, not the social, world. (Even abstract art abstracts from natural phenomena.) This linkage to the natural world allows us clearer access to see how an "in-visible" is born out of the visible which is not a *de facto* invisible as the cup which is hidden from view by the cupboard; nor is it an absolute invisible which would have nothing to do with the visible world.[6] Merleau-Ponty quotes da Vinci's *Treatise on Painting*:

> The secret of the art of drawing is to discover in each object the particular way in which a certain flexuous line, which is, so to speak its generating axis, is directed through its whole extent . . ." (EM p. 183),

For Merleau-Ponty, Da Vinci in the quote above intimates the bond between the visible and the invisible. The discovery of "single flexuous line" is a creation of an "in-visible" from the visible. It henceforth becomes a means by which the object may be seen. Van Gogh's repeated painting of a single chair reveals a similar creating of an "in-visible." Van Gogh, in returning to this subject did not mean to substitute its physical presence with a superior or more remarkable view. The "invisible" is not an imitation, representation or idealization of the object. And Van Gogh, in Merleau-Ponty's view, did not express an "inner schema" which the physical object unleashed from Van Gogh's own psyche. Rather, the painter's vision uncovers hidden configurations and framework for which the natural world does not fail to provide abundant ground and resources. As Merleau-Ponty states it, the painter's vision occurs when "an operant and latent meaning finds the emblems which are going to disengage it and make it manageable for the artist and at the same time accessible to others." (*Signs* p. 53). Merleau-Ponty again searches for original language to express the relation between the "in-visible" and the visible. He employs such expressions as "an absence circumscribed" (VI p. 151; *VI* p. 198), a "certain interior", a "certain hollow" (VI. p. 151; *VI* p. 198) and more frequently "an invisible of this world" (VI P. 151; *VI* p. 198). These expressions imply the "in" of systematic difference and stress that the index is hidden but implied by the visible.

In a manner which seems bizarre at first, Merleau-Ponty extends the notion of flesh to entities in general. There is a "flesh of things," he states. (VI p. 133; *VI* p. 175)

> The red dress a fortiori holds with all its fibers onto the fabric of the visible, and thereby onto a fabric of invisible being . . . a naked color and in general a visible, is not a chunk of absolutely hard indivisible being, offered all naked to a vision which could be only total or null, but it is rather a straits between exterior and interior horizons ever gaping open . . . less a color or a thing therefore, than a difference between things, a momentary crystallization of colored being or of visibility. (VI p. 132; *VI* p. 174–5)

In speaking of a flesh of things Merleau-Ponty emphasizes a way of thinking of things which is to some extent already conveyed in our ordinary use of "flesh." When we speak of seeing someone "in the flesh" we imply that we directly confront a person's essential style. We imply that we see a person fully. Yet in speaking of the flesh we also speak of an entity which is particularly real by virtue of what it keeps hidden; it shows itself by reference to what is unseen. The red dress in the quote above exemplifies this vision of things. For us to see the red in the full richness of a particular red dress, we also see by implication a variety of other reds which it hides.

Again the schema of an index upon a field of differences is relevant. But we must stress that Merleau-Ponty describes a vision of things wherein they are most fully presented. Neitzsche in *Beyond Good and Evil* states that one might describe, instead of true and false appearances, "grades of apparentness and as it were lighter and darker shades and tones of appearance— different *valeurs* to speak the language of painters."[7] Merleau-Ponty's notion of flesh is a way of describing things in extreme "apparentness" or vividness. His account of flesh is a vision of things appearing in maximal "apparentness." The phrase above wherein he states that the certain red is "a straits between interior and exterior horizons" is to the same purpose. Interior and exterior horizons imply a manifest figure in relation to an unimposing background. As we have indicated, however, he has revised the horizonal concept of field. The relation between hidden and exposed is such that the hidden imposes itself upon our vision as powerfully as the exposed. The thing implies other objects as differences in the way that flesh—in our ordinary sense of flesh—maintains its power through what is never made naked. Flesh as flesh is never fully naked yet always implies nakedness, not as a background but as an "in-visible" in Merleau-Ponty's sense.

Any instance of the flesh counts as an "installation" of the chiasm relation for Merleau-Ponty and its extension is as broad. One has an instance of the flesh whenever a level is maintained as an index of difference within a field. Consequently one can have a "flesh as expression." (VI p. 145; *VI* p. 190) as well as a "flesh of the world." (VI p. 248; *VI* p. 302) A celebrated double entendre in *The Marriage of Figaro* might serve to exemplify how expression is given "in the flesh." In the Second Act, Mozart has the Count order: "Donna mi la chiava," that is, "give me the key." The Count wants the key to a locked door where he thinks, the page, Cherubino is hiding. The Count believes that Cherubino has seduced the Countess. When he is given the key to the door, Mozart playfully also gives him the key, i. e. the tonality of that musical episode. Mozart makes sport here of the notion of musical key but also suggests its deeper sense. The key is a means of entrance. The physical key allows the Count to unlock the door to the Countess' chambers. Once the Count has the key he appears fully for what he is— much to the chagrin of the Countess and the page, Cherubino. But the *musical* key is also a means of entrance. When the tone is given we are led into the new aria. The tone allows the aria to appear as an organized musical composition. The boldness and strength of the aria are revealed in relation the tonal center. In Merleau-Ponty's terms, the key, E-flat major, is a level which operates again as an index in the system of differences, i. e. the notes of the aria. The aria is a "coherent deformation or deviation" from the key note. The key is also a tone, albeit an index tone. It can also take its place among the other tones in the aria. We are reminded how illumination, itself a color can become a level by which the color spectrum is discerned. And as we have seen before, the notion of levels is not approached as a "positive significance." A level marks a pervasive difference in a field of differences. The language of levels plays further into the integration of Merleau-Ponty's later thought insofar as it enables him to specify the manner of difference or separation in the chiasm relation.

The "petite phrase" described in *Un amour de Swann* is also an example of the "flesh of expression." Here the "field" is as broad as the multitude of recollections of the two lovers, Swann and Odette. "No one has gone further than Proust," Merleau-Ponty tells us "in fixing the relations between the visible and the invisible, in describing an idea that is not contrary of the sensible, that it is its lining and depth." (VI p. 149; *VI* p. 195) Proust, in recounting the conversations, meetings, plans, encounters and intimacies of Swann and Odette, introduces the petite phrase as a marker. In his descriptions it signals shifts in the development of Swann and Odette's love. It is present at their meeting and is involved with setting the mood of their first encounter. It becomes a favorite piece of Odette's and she plays it for Swann in intimate settings. It comes to be incorporated into their private responses and intimacies. Consequently, the little phrase comes to have bearing upon the whole of Swann's and

Odette's love affair. Proust prepares an extraordinary moment of recognition through the hearing of this phrase. Swann realizes that his affair with Odette has ended when he hears the little phrase in the Vinteuil Sonata at a evening at Saint-Euverte. The phrase recaptures for him the course of his love for Odette. It gives him access to his love affair and as such allows him to envisage its consequences.[8] How is the phrase an instance of flesh? Proust understood that the phrase was not separate from Swann and Odette's love. It did not present the love affair in condensation or simulation. The phrase provided a key to the recollection of the love affair since from the beginning it marked the differences in its course.

We may define the flesh, then as follows: "Flesh" is a style of being, manifested by the chiasm relation, and embodying a relation between a level, as a coherent index of differentiation, and a field, given as coherent differences from a level. Aspects of Merleau-Ponty's concept agree with our ordinary usage. When we see someone "in the flesh" we are indicating that we fully see that person; essential aspects of their style are implied in their "here and now" behavior. We are also indicating that not immediately present aspects of the person—actions or capacities we have heard of—pervade their "here and now behavior." Flesh, even in our ordinary usage, then, implies an imposing and co-present hiddenness. Merleau-Ponty applies his revised notion of field to the phenomenon of flesh. A person is given in the flesh insofar as the person's behavior is an index within a field of differences. Furthermore, Merleau-Ponty fully makes the flesh into an ontological element. There is a flesh of expression as well as a flesh of the world. Here the pliability and expressiveness contained in our ordinary sense of flesh is extended to suggest how any entity implies both a "here and now" aspect as well as a level or norm which suggest how it is one manner of variation. The notion of the flesh directs us to a particularly vivid or manifest appearance of a thing or expression.

In passing, we might note that offering a definition of the flesh is problematic. The flesh as well as the chiasma relation, Merleau-Ponty insists, cannot be thought as a "positive signification." Thought which posits, places or sets up an idea among others as one place an object among others is not appropriate for these notions. Fields of differences, just because they never imply any object except as a difference from another object do not fit a mode of conceptualization which would make an object central. In the next section in this chapter, we will explicate the problem of conceptualizing the chiasm and the flesh as objects. I shall argue that this cannot be done inasmuch as they are not available to "representational thinking."

3. The unavailability of Merleau-Ponty's later thought to representational thinking—

The notion of the flesh along with Merleau-Ponty's later ontology in general is not available to representational thinking. I have taken the term, "representational thinking" from Heidegger's *Discourse on Thinking* where Heidegger describes conventional thinking as representational. In this section, I shall quote from that dialogue at some length. Merleau-Ponty is aware that his later work requires a radical shift in a manner of thinking. He himself grapples with a shift in thinking in *The Visible and the Invisible* and admits to providing philosophical descriptions in a manner which is no longer suitable.

Heidegger in his *Discourse on Thinking*, German title, *Gelassenheit*, offers a characterization of what he takes to be "the traditional view of the nature of thinking."[9] The following dialogue is quoted in full from a passage in that work:[10]

Scientist: Previously, we had come to see thinking in the form of transcendental-horizonal representing.

Scholar: This re-presenting, for instance, places before us what is typical of a tree, of a pitcher, of a bowl, or a stone, of plants, and of animals as that view into which we look when one thing confronts us in the appearance of a tree, another thing in the appearance of a pitcher, this in the appearance of a bowl, various things in the appearance of plants, and many in the appearance of animals.

Scientist: You describe, once again, the horizon which encircles the thing—the field of vision.

Teacher: It goes beyond the appearance of objects.

Scholar: Just as transcendence passes beyond the perception of objects.

Teacher: Thus we determine what is called horizon and transcendence by means of this going beyond and passing beyond . . .

Scholar: . . . which refer back to objects and our representing of objects.

Teacher: Horizon and transcendence, thus are experienced and determined only relative to objects and our representing them.

Scholar: Why do you stress this?

Teacher: To suggest that in this way what lets the horizon be what it has not yet been encountered at all.

Scientist: What do you have in mind in this statement?

Teacher: We say that we look into the horizon. Therefore the field of vision is something open, but its openness is not due to our looking.

Scholar: Likewise we do not place the appearance of objects, which the view within the field of vision offers us, into this openness . . .

Scientist: . . . rather that comes out of this to meet us.

In Heidegger's view traditional thinking "re-presents" objects. This means that thinking presents them again through reflecting on what is typical of the objects. A thinking subject makes the representation of objects, as the presentation of objects, into the work of a central subject which summons, organizes and scrutinizes objects. The world of thought, like the world of objects, is organized around a central subject which are as so many utensils or pieces of equipment arranged around a craftsman. The result is that thinking is presumed to have a particular context: we understand ourselves to be central and to draw thought from the world around us which is understood as peripheral to us. If metaphors help, the accomplishment of thinking follows in our wake like so many figures formed upon water by the movement of a boat passing over it.

In Heidegger's account this concept of thinking, which models thinking upon a relation to objects, bears the faults and prejudices of the implied theory of objects. Within a tradition that makes the presence of objects "due to our looking," we correspondingly make thinking the product of a thinking subject and "due to our thinking." Furthermore it is presumed that thinking, like the positioning of objects in a perceptual field which is conceived as an expanse around us, "posits," "places" or "sets up" one notion in relation to another notion as one might place set up or arrange objects in relation to one another. A manner of thinking which involves an "approaching," "coming," "nearing" or "opening" of significations which are formed, as it were, within their own context is alien to the expectations and conditions of traditional thinking. Now it is this second kind of thinking that Merleau-Ponty's later thought calls upon. We must stress that instances of the chiasm relation or of flesh cannot be *posited* or *placed* in space as objects can be placed in a room. They in fact do not presuppose a spatial context. For representational thinking such notions are simply not sensible. Traditional representational thinking is rather like the ordinary illumination by which we see things in the world. Yet there are entities which cannot be seen by this illumination and which nonetheless are available within other illuminations as infra-red photography reveals markings on insects that have long been operating as stimuli although we could not perceive them through the light of the spectrum. In demanding that he cease thinking of entities as *positive* and think instead of them as *differentiations* (VI p. 270; *VI* p. 324) Merleau-Ponty is suggesting that dismissing the former means of conceptualizing is a requirement for approaching the issues he wishes to treat. Or to return to our metaphor again, the chiasm relation and the relation of the visible to the invisible cannot be thought of as a relation between *positive* entities any more than sunlight can expose the full color markings of a Monarch butterfly.

It appears clear that Merleau-Ponty himself is not altogether at home with the requirements of his later thought. He himself is grappling with the radical shift which is required. After offering the metaphor of leaves, and later more literally, of layers to describe the "sentient/sensible" sides of the body, for example, he states he had best retract these terms.

> One should not even say, as we did a moment ago, that the body is made up of two leaves, of which the one, that of the "sensible," is bound up with the rest of the world. There are not in it two leaves or two layers; fundamentally it is neither thing seen only nor seer only, it is Visibility sometimes wandering and sometime assembled. And as such it is not in the world . . . (VI p. 137-8; *VI* p. 183)

The problem in speaking of leaves or layers, or in general as is his worry in another passage, in "thinking by planes and perspectives" (VI p. 138; *VI* p. 182) is that these highly visual notions invite us to relate them to a spatial positioning which sets them around us as we might place objects around us. Accordingly, the sentient side of the body is somehow placed next, opposite, or alongside the sensible side of the body. But if we think of the "sides" of the body along these lines we shall never catch the interrelationship Merleau-Ponty wishes to describe. (Nor we might add will we understand Heidegger's view of thinking which in his view is definitive of human being.) Thinking of the sides of the body, or in general of the mind to the body as levels and differences calls for more than applying foreign notions to areas to which we are surprised to find they have applications. It requires that the spatial context which we take for granted in the positing and placing of objects be accepted as irrelevant. This involves a departure from a habitual form of conceiving and understanding whose proportions one ought not to underestimate.

The sides of the chiasm relation are "in" one other to the extent that we cannot think one without implying the other. But this does not mean that we cannot posit one without another. It is more that the "in" in this sense entails that the other is "in the vicinity" or "is near" the other. The distances involved are distances according to meaning, not according to separations in space. The shock of the woman's heel referred to in Section 2

152

may be connected to a recollection of a gesture that took place months before. The sound of the heel nonetheless is "in" that recollection along with a host of others. We have already discussed the importance of distinguishing usages of "in." But it is important to see now that the thinking that we are called on to accept is alien to a spatial context altogether. By what concept of spatiality are we to relate the closeness of the sense of "in" we are discussing? Accordingly, when we say that the side of the chiasm relation are "in" one another, we are not implying that we as thinkers have this perspective or view. This again invites us to think in terms of a spatial context and in fact puts us as thinkers into a position of centrality. In perceiving an instance of the flesh, our role as thinkers is not central but "participatory." In the broadest sense this is implied by Merleau-Ponty's intention to revise being-in-the-world in favor of a belonging to Being. He implies our participatory relation to the flesh or chiasm often. As he states, for example, ". . . he who sees cannot possess the visible unless he is possessed of it, unless he is *of it*. (VI p. 134; *VI* p. 177–8) We approach or near a particular instance of sides of the chiasm relation. When it is open to us we are "of it." We are surrounded by it and we cannot help but play some role in the situation which is opened to us.

In dealing with Merleau-Ponty's later thought, we are required to follow the implications of such odd terminology as "dehiscence." Among other purposes, his use of such terms helps us to shift to another mode of thinking. Apart from those who are familiar with botanical nomenclature, the term will likely appear foreign. As with the chiasm, Merleau-Ponty, in all likelihood, is worried about the extent to which conventional terms invite conventional approaches. So he turns to unusual sources. In botany "dehiscence" signifies the manner in which seeds burst from a seed-pod. The seed-pod bursts leaving its various parts split, yet present together on the same stalk. The metaphor is a good one. Again it stresses difference or separation in the elemental sense Merleau-Ponty wants to give to it. It also suggests the beginning of some new thing. The seeds are evident from this small biological explosion. Finally if we are to gain access to thinking according to difference—not by positing theses or views—we need to take the notion of dehiscience or the special sense he brings to *ecart* as capable of generating an orientation which is otherwise alien to us. In my opinion there is no question of preference in relation to these two styles of thinking. But there is an opposition which invites a misunderstanding of his efforts and likely obscures how this manner of thinking can lead to successes in further investigations. One line of thinking excludes the other. One presumes a spatial context; the other does not. Consequently as soon as one supposes the conditions of the first brand of thinking, the possible successes of the second disappear. At least, then, insofar as one is initiated into a new manner of thinking which applies not only to Merleau-Ponty's thought but to what might well amount to an viable alternative approach to issues or solutions beyond the context of his philosophy, we may acknowledge the value of the exhortation that recurrently appears in his later writings: "all this bric-a-brac, is suddenly clarified when one ceases to think of these terms as *positive* . . . but as *differentiations* of one sole and *massive* adhesion to Being . . ." (VI p. 270; *VI* p. 324)

4. Further regions of the flesh and the chiasm: a new approach to the philosophy of history and mind.

Besides offering an indirect ontology in *The Visible and the Invisible*, Merleau-Ponty intended to criticize conceptual presuppositions in psychology, social theory and history as well as philosophy. Our intention in this chapter extends primarily to explicating the chiasm in its "element," the flesh, and finally to expose the difficulties entailed in thinking such notions along conventional lines. These notions, however, are readily applicable to main areas of philosophy. Much of the sketching of applications was already accomplished in Merleau-Ponty's later works. In this last section I would like to extend the notion of the chiasm and the flesh by filling out these sketches in two main areas. First Merleau-Ponty's later approach to the philosophy of mind; and second his treatment of a philosophy of history.

154

—a sketch for a new philosophy of history—

Michel Foucault writes in *The Archeology of Knowledge*:[11]

> By *episteme* we mean . . . the total set of relations that unite, at a given period, the discursive practices that gives rise to epistemological figures, sciences, and possibly formalized systems . . . The episteme is not a form of knowledge (*connaissance*) or type of rationality which, crossing the boundaries of the most varied sciences, manifests the soveriegn of a subject, a spirit, or a period, it is the totality of relations that can be discovered, for a given period, between the sciences when one analyzes them at the level of discursive regularities.

Foucault attended Merleau-Ponty's lectures at the Sorbonne and was aware first hand of his later views.[12] In the quote above, Foucault indicates that he has developed the approach to history that Merleau-Ponty sketches in his later works. We may note an overlap between the two thinkers' thought as revealed through Foucault's fundamental notion of an *episteme*. An *episteme* is an unformalized discursive practice. It suggests Merleau-Ponty's later approach to history wherein thought cannot be extracted from social practices. In the *Visible and the Invisible*, for example, he describes practices so profoundly wedded to the culture that any "thesis made of it amounts to an idealization." (VI p. 94; *VI* p. 129)

Merleau-Ponty's later ontology implies grounds for revising the notion of "historicity." There is no question of positing a supervening Reason or Mind in history. We need not choose between understanding the arrival of capitalism, for example, materialistically, or understanding it as a stage in the dialectic of Mind. If one is to understand the presence of capitalism in a society, one needs to understand how a culture can be interwoven with "situational thoughts." (VI p. 92; *VI* p. 126) Merleau-Ponty suggests the notion of a "hyper-dialectic" (VI pp. 94–5; *VI* p. pp. 129–30), not a shift to an antithesis which follows through the design of Mind or materialism. These approaches remove us from the linkage that a particular practice has in things and from the manner in which we are drawn by a culture into a practice. In a particular historical epoch circumstances "lend themselves" to a singular interpretation.

We may recognize here again the fundamental notions of the chiasm and flesh. As he tells us "we would undoubtedly recover the concept of history in the true sense of the term if we were to get used to modeling it after the example of the arts and language. (*Signs* p. 73) The style of social practice is as present in the society as the painter's vision is in his work. A culture draws itself to "that risky position" of sustaining a certain cultural practice. (*Signs* p. 69) Circumstances incline themselves to the creation of a practice, as the "diversity of parts of the body gather themselves into a gesture which dominates their dispersion and put a stamp on it." (*Signs* p. 68) We have a historical version of the chiasm relation. But in so saying we understand that one is never confronted with a meaning which is unchangeable. To be sure, there is no question of extrapolation, surpassing, or adding a negation, nor of a synthesis. The notion of a movement to history is already rooted in the overall shift in signification as difference. One historical epoch is given as dovetailing with another just because it is given as different from another. Because the cultural solution that has been struck is an approach to the world, and "hollowed out" from it and because we have a social practice which is given as a difference, we are lodged in a historical situation from which, as he states, "we know that something new will come to pass, even if it is only the end of this life which has barely begun." (*Signs* p. 69)

—a sketch for a new philosophy of mind—

Define the mind as the other side of the body—. . . There is a body of a mind and a mind of the body and a chiasm between them. (VI p. 259; *VI p. 312–3*)

In Merleau-Ponty's later ontology, the mind is "in" the body in the sense of an "in-visible" in the visible. The notion of flesh implies its own manner of interiority and exteriority. If we confuse the "in" of an index in a field of differences with the "in" of containment we will engender traditional confusions of thinking that a person's mind is in his body in the sense that liquid is in a cup. On the other hand, if we take mind to be the institution of levels, there is no longer difficulty in understanding how mental phenomena can be "adherent to location and the now" (VI p. 140; *VI* p. 193) while *at the same time* intimating a systemic relation to a field.

In a Working Note dated December 1960, Merleau-Ponty indicated that the notion of the flesh was to explicate a number of psychological concepts which traditionally are conceived along the lines of mental or bodily entities where mind and body are given a "positive significance."

> The whole architecture of the notion of the psycho-logy (perception, idea—affection, pleasure, desire, love, and Eros) all that, all this bric-a-brac, is suddenly clarified when one ceases to think all these terms as *positive* (More or less dense "spiritual") in order to think them not as negatives or negentities (for that brings back the same difficulties), but as *differentiations* of one sole *massive* adhesion to Being, which is the flesh . . . (VI p. 270)

We can discern through this citation the scope of what was to become Merleau-Ponty's later philosophy of mind. First in reference to the notion of the unconscious. Insofar as the unconscious is referred to as a type of mind, we are led to distinguish it from the conscious or sub-conscious mind. One feature which has been attributed to the unconscious mind since Freud is its capacity to express itself in symbols which reveal a multitude of significances. The unconscious mind, unlike the conscious mind, as it shows itself in dreams, slips or neurotic behavior, provides symbols which are "overdetermined."

The notion of the unconscious mind as overdetermined occurs often in Freud's writings. Freud discovered in the symptoms, dreams or screen memories, a condensation of meanings. He attributed this condensation to the unconscious mind. The symbols engendered by the unconscious were called "overdetermined" since the degree of allusions which are condensed in the symbol does not admit the possibility of being wholly

157

enumerated or "unpacked." In a note, for example, Merleau-Ponty refers to Freud's description of one of his patients described in *The Psychopathology of Everyday Life*. (VI. p. 241; *VI* p. 294). The patient dreams of an *Espe* which is associated with a wasp. This symbol, so it would seem, represents a classic case of overdetermination. The patient's initials are S. P. The word "espe" is further associated with a shortened form of "Wespe," i. e. "wasp." It suggests a wasp whose wings, like a "W" were pulled off. Freud interprets the symbol as expressive of the patient's castration fear. The symbol expresses this fear in a multitude of manners: the broken word i. e. the removal of the W from the rest of the word, the symbolization of the figure of the "W," the pulling off of the wasp's wings, etc. We are left to reflect on an unconscious mind which overdetermines the symbols it makes use of.

What is wrong with this manner of describing the unconscious? From Merleau-Ponty's point of view, there are two main confusions involved. The first involves distinguishing the unconscious from the conscious mind through the notion of over-determination. The second applies to the notion of mind altogether and involves a model of mind wherein it is taken to be a subject which ranges or surveys one's experience.

First, in Merleau-Ponty's view, "Overdetermination always occurs." (VI p. 240; *VI* p. 294) It is not only a feature of the unconscious mind, it is also a feature of the conscious mind and in general of the flesh. In the case of the unconscious mind there is a flattening of temporal extension but the feature of overdetermination is no less present in ordinary consciousness. The dreamer's symbol, the wasp and the word "Espe" count as a symbol because it avails itself of the requisite pairing of a level with a field of differences. The overall structure is not different from what we have already encountered. The relation of Swann's little phrase to his love affair with Odette is also overdetermined. Swann himself, it is likely, would not be able to recall all of the experiences which were introduced and operate in his final hearing of the little phrase. In a sense the unconscious mind shows its uncanny powers of symbolization since when we reflect upon it we are more conscious of the relation of levels to fields although we do not understand its symbolizing in those terms.

For Merleau-Ponty, the conscious mind no more ranges over a separable field of significances which is present to it than the unconscious does. Merleau-Ponty in fact means to dismantle the notion of consciousness altogether as a positive entity which is distinct from objects.

> One does not get out of the rationalism-irrationalism dilemma as long as one thinks "consciousness" and "acts"—The decisive step is to realize that in fact consciousness is intentionality without acts . . . that the "objects" of consciousness themselves are not something positive *in front of* us, but nuclei of signification about which the transcendental life pivots . . . (VI p. 238–9; *VI* p. 292)

Again a key phrase in the quote above is "not something positive." As he repeatedly states the mind cannot be described in objective thought. The mind as a whole is a dimensionality, "a transcendence of the negative toward the sensible." (VI p. 259; *VI* p. 313) By this we are to understand that if fully unravelled we would find that the mind is the dimensional side of a chiasm relation. There is no question of mind as a positive entity distinct from the body. It is rather a question of levels struck in the perception of an object, mannerisms, use-objects or speech. In Merleau-Ponty's later view the whole system of conceptual apparatus which would see the mind as made of intentions, desires, needs, projects, drives—various manners of directedness towards the world—are rethought as levels. These notions which have been treated as positive entities are taken to be part of the system of differences. Let us consider how this applies to a theory of drives, for example. Freud held that there are four "psychosexual objects" which one becomes fixated on in childhood. They serve to create various character types depending on the fixation. He designated oral, anal, phallic and genital fixations. A fixation on breast-feeding, for example, which engenders the "oral personality" gives rise to such traits as loquaciousness, over-eating, chain-smoking, etc. all in view of the pleasures which have become fixated on the mouth. Freud associated drives with these psycho-sexual objects by which an individual maintained his fixation or "cathexis."

The first problem with this account is that it becomes difficult to see how a single fixation can affect systematically the individual's dealing with a multitude of various objects in the world. If however one sees the fixation not as a relation between a drive and an object, but instead a way of organizing one's world which leads the thing to be a "light," so to speak, by which all things are seen, dealt with, acted upon, etc. it becomes clear how the so-called oral fixation can assume its breadth in one's behavior. For the oral-fixated man, the world suggests a manner of behavior for which orality is the solution. It again is a level which organizes a collection of activities each one significant by its thematic difference. The oral drive or the oral fixation, then, amounts to an insertion in the world, as an "invisible of this world" which reveals a certain predeliction for "the soft side of life."

Secondly, the pairing of drives with a fixed set of objects misses that "any entity can be accentuated as an emblem of Being." (VI p. 269; *VI* p. 323) To the extent that Freud misses this, he really comes to be at a loss to explain how a single person can be a dimension or level. It is a common enough experience that we can fall in love with a single person to the extent that this person becomes "the measure of all things," and as such, the main source of pleasure and delight. If the four objects Freud mentions were the only objects that could be fixated, it would follow that any woman, for the breast-fixated individual, would do. But of course Eros is not quite so democratic. Once Eros is conceived as a dimension taken upon the world, the manner in which this psychological entity is immersed in our world becomes remarkably clear. Eros is a version of the flesh of the world wherein a thing or person is taken to be a measure of our world and leads us thereby to find in that person or thing a measure of the rest.

160

Notes To Chapter Four

[1] Browning, Robert, *The Collected Works*. Volume Ten, Earnest Benn Ltd., 1912, London, p. 163, ("Parleyings with Certain People," Bernard de Mandeville, lines 190–1)

[2] Heverkamp-Begemann, E., *Rembrandt: The Nightwatch*, Princeton University Press, 1982, Princeton, p. 113

[3] Wallace, Robert, *The World of Rembrandt*, Time-Life Books, New York, 1968, p. 110

[4] Husserl, Edmund, *Husserliana: Cartesianische Meditationen* p. 128 and *Ideen II*, p. 145.

[5] The notion of mirroring in the formation of the self occurs recurrently in Kohut's writings. For an introduction to his views on the formation of the self see his "Remarks About the Formation of the Self" as it appears in *The Search for the Self*, edited by Paul H. Ornstein, International Universities Press, Inc., 1978, New York.

[6] See VI p. 151; *VI* p. 198 for a discussion of three kinds of invisibility.

[7] Nietzsche, F, *Beyond Good and Evil*, Section 34, Hollingsdale translation, Penguin Books, New York, 1973, p. 47

[8] Proust's description of this episode are among the finest of his work. We do injustice to the literary merit of the section by taking a passage from the context. But passages such as the following do indicate how Proust is aware that a few notes can "render visible" as he says countless occasions.

> Those graces of an intimate sorrow, it was them that the phrase endeavored to imitate, to create anew; and even their essence, for all that it consists in being incommunicable and in appearing trivial to everyone save him who has experience of them, the little phrase had captured and rendered visible.

Proust, Marcel, *Remembrance of Things Past*, Montcrieff translation, Random House, 1934, New York, p. 267

[9] Heidegger, Martin, *Discourse on Thinking* translation by Anderson and Freund, Harper Colophon Books, New York, 1966, p. 63

[10] Ibid. pp. 63–4

[11] Foucault, Michel, *The Archeology of Knowledge*, translated by Sheridan Smith, New York, Harper Colophon, 1972, p. 191

[12] See Dreyfus, H. L. and Rabinow, Paul, *Michel Foucault: Beyond Structuralism and Hermeneutics*, University of Chicago Press, Chicago, 1982, pp xviiff for Merleau-Ponty's influence on Foucault.

Bibliography

Works by Merleau-Ponty in French

Merleau-Ponty, Maurice, *Les aventures de la dialectique*, Paris. 1955, Gallimard.
———, *Éloge de la philosophie*, Paris, Gallimard, 1953.
———, *Humanisme et terreur*, Paris, 1947, Gallimard
———, *L'Oeil et l'esprit*, Paris, Gallimard, 1964.
———, *Phénoménologie de la perception*, Paris, Gallimard, 1945.
———, 'Le Primat de la perception et ses consequences philosophies,' *Bulletin de la Société Francaise de Philosophie*, 41:4, October-December, 1947.
———, *La Prose du monde*, Paris, Gallimard, 1969.
———, *Résumé de Cours*: *College de France, 1952–1960*, Paris, Gallimard, 1968.
———, *Sens et non-sens*, Paris, Nagel, 1948.
———, *Signes*, Paris, Gallimard, 1960.
———, *La Structure de comportement*, Paris, Presses Universitaires de France, Sixth Edition, 1967.
———, *Le Visible et l'invisible*, Paris, Gallimard, 1964.

English Translations of Works by Merleau-Ponty

Merleau-Ponty, Maurice, *Adventures of the Dialectic*, Translated by Joseph Bien, Northwestern University Press, 1973, Evanston.
———, *Consciousness and the Acquisition of Language*, notes from lectures given at the Sorbonne 1949–51, translated by Hugh J. Silverman, Northwestern University Press, Evanston, 1973.
———, *Humanism and Terror*, translated by J. O'Neill, Beason Press, 1969, Boston.
———, *In Praise of Philosophy*, translation by John Wild and James Edie, Northwestern University Press, 1963, Evanston, Ill.
———, *The Phenomenology of Perception*, translation by Colin Smith, revised by Forrest Williams, London, 1962, Routledge & Kegan Paul.
———, *The Primacy of Perception*, translation by James Edie, Northwestern University Press, 1964, Evanston, Ill.
———, *The Prose of the World*, translation by John O'Neill, Northwestern University Press, 1973, Evanston, Ill.
———, *Sense and Non-Sense*, translation by Hubert Dreyfus and Patricia Dreyfus, Northwestern University Press, 1964, Evanston, Ill.

——, *Signs*, translation by Richard McCleary, Northwestern University Press, 1964, Evanston, Ill.

——, *The Structure of Behavior*, translation by Alden Fisher, Beacon Press, Second paperback printing, 1968, Boston.

——, *The Visible and the Invisible*, translation by Alphonso Lingis, Northwestern University Press, 1968, Evanston, Ill.

Secondary Sources

Alquie Ferdinand, 'Une Philosophy de l'ambiguité: L'Existentialisme de Merleau-Ponty,' *Fontaine*, 11:59 (April, 1947), pp. 47–70.

Aristotle, *Metaphysics*, translation by W. D. Ross, many editions.

Bachelard, Gaston, *The Poetics of Space*, translation by Maria Jolas, Beacon Press, 1969, Boston.

Ballard, Edward G., 'On Cognition of the Pre-Cognitive—Merleau-Ponty,' *Philosophical Quarterly*, 11:44 (July, 1961), pp. 238–44.

Bergson, Henrin, *Matter and Memory*, translation by Hulme, New York, Putnam and Sons, 1913. Reprinted in paperback by the Liberal Arts Press, 1949.

Dreyfus, Hubert L., *Husserl's Phenomenology of Perception: From Transcendental Phenomenology to Existentialism*, a dissertation written in preparation for doctorate, Harvard University.

Dreyfus, Hubert L., and S.J. Todes, 'The Three Worlds of Merleau-Ponty' *Philosophy and Phenomenological Research*, 22:4 (June, 1962).

Fink, Eugen, "Der phänomenolische Philosophie Edmund Husserls in der gegenwärtigen Kritik," translated by R. O. Elveton and appearing in his collection, *The Phenomenology of Edmund Husserl*, Quadrangle Books, 1970, Chicago.

Foucault, Michel, *A History of Sexuality. Vol. I: An Introduction*, 1980, Random House, New York.

——, *Discipline and Punish: The Birth of the Prison*, A. Sheridan translator, Random House, 1979, New York.

Gillian, Garth, editor, *The Horizons of the Flesh*, a collection of essays on Merleau-Ponty, Southern Illinois University Press, 1973, Carbondale, Ill.

Granel, G., *Le sens du temps et de la perception chez E Husserl*, Gallimard, Paris, 1968, p. 103.

Gurwitsch, Aron, *The Field of Consciousness*, Dusquesne University Press, 1964, Pittsburgh.

Hamlyn, D. W., *Sensation and Perception: A History of the Philosophy of Perception*, The Humanities Press, 1961, London.

Hegel, G. W. F., *The Phenomenology of the Spirit*, translation by Miller, Clarendon Press, Oxford, 1977.

Heidsieck, Francois, *L'Ontologie de Merleau-Ponty*, Presses Universitaires de France, 1971, Paris.

Heidegger, Martin, *Being and Time*, translation by Macquarrie and Robinson, Harper and Bros., 1962, New York.

——, *Discourse on Thinking*, Harper & Row, New York, 1966.

——, *On the Way to Language*, translated by P. D. Hertz, Harper and Row, 1971, New York.

——, *Poetry, Language and Thought*, translated by Albert Hofstadter, Harper and Row, 1971, New York.

——, *The Question Concerning Technology and Other Essays*, Harper and Row, New York, 1977.

——, *Identity and Difference*, translation by Joan Stambaugh, Harper and Row, 1969, New York.

Heverkamp-Begemann, E., *Rembrandt: The Nightwatch*, Princeton University Press, 1982, Princeton.

Husserl, Edmund, *The Cartesian Meditations*, translation by Dorian Cairns, Martinus Nijhoff, 1952, The Hague.

——, *The Crisis of European Sciences and Transcendental Phenomenology*, translation by David Carr, Northwestern University Press, 1970, Evanston Ill.

——, *Erfahrung und Urteil, Untersuchen zur Genealogie der Logik*, edited by L. Landgrebe, Academia Verlagsbuchhandlungen, 1939, Prague.

——, *Formal and Transcendental Logic*, translated by Dorions Cairns, The Hague, Martinus Nijhoff, 1969.

——, *Ideas*, translation by W. R. Boyce Gibson, Macmillan Co., 1958, New York.

——, *Logical Investigations*, Findlay translation, Routledge & Kegan Paul, London, 1970.

Hyppolite, Jean, *Sens et existence dans la philosophie de Maurice Merleau-Ponty*, The Zaharoff Lecture for 1963, The Clarendon Press, 1963, Oxford.

Koffka, Kurt, *Principles of Gestalt Psychology*, Harcourt, Brace and Co., 1935, New York.

Kohut, Heinz, *The Search for the Self*, edited by Paul Ornstein, International Universities Press, Inc., 1978, New York.

Koestler, Arthur and Smythies, J. R., editors, *Beyond Reductionism*, Beacon Press, 1969, Boston.

Kwant, Remy C., *The Phenomenological Philosophy of Merleau-Ponty*, translation by Henry J. Koren, Dusquesne University Press, 1963, Pittsburgh.

Langan, Thomas, *Merleau-Ponty's Critique of Reason*, Yale University Press, 1966, New Haven.

Madison, Gary Brent, *The Phenomenology of Merleau-Ponty*, Ohio University Press, Athens, Ohio, 1981.

Mallin, Samuel B., *Merleau-Ponty's Philosophy*, Yale University Press, New Haven, 1979.

Marcel, Gabriel, *Metaphysical Journal*, translation by Bernard Wall, Henry Regnery Co., 1952, Chicago.

Mehta, J. L., *Martin Heidegger: The Way and the Vision*, University Press of Hawaii, 1976.

Nietzsche, F., *Thus Spake Zarathustra*, T. Common translator, Modern Library Edition, 1927, New York.

Paget, *Human Speech*, Routledge & Kegan Paul Ltd., London, 1963.

Plato, *The Cratylus*, Jowett translation, Random House, New York, 1937.

Proust, Marcel, *A Remembrance of Things Past*, Montcrieff translation, Random House, 1934, New York.

Rabil, Albert, Jr., *Merleau-Ponty: Existentialist of the Social World*, Columbia University Press, 1967, New York.

164

Richardson, William J., *Heidegger, Through Phenomenology to Thought*, Martinus Nijhoff, 1967, The Hague.

Rorty, Richard, *Philosophy and the Mirror of Nature*, Princeton University Press, 1979, Princeton.

Sartre, Jean-Paul, *Being and Nothingness*, translation by Hazel Barnes, Philosophical Library, 1956, New York.

———, 'Merleau-Ponty vivant,' *Les Temps Modernes*, 17:184–5 (October, 1961), 304–76.

———, *The Transcendance of the Ego*, translation by Forest Williams and Robert Kirkpatrick, The Noonday Press, 1962, New York.

Scheler, Max, *Man's Place in Nature*, translation by Hans Meyerhoff, The Noonday Press, 1971, New York.

Spiegelberg, Herbert, *The Phenomenological Movement: A Historical Introduction*. Martinus Nijhoff, 1960, The Hague.

Strasser, Stephan, *Phenomenology and the Human Sciences*, translation by Henry J. Koren, Dusquesne University Press, 1963, Pittsburgh.

Tilliette, Xavier, *Merleau-Ponty ou la mesure de l'homme*, Philosophies de tous les temps, 1970, Paris.

Van Bread, H.L., 'Maurice Merleau-Ponty et les Archives-Husserl à Louvain,' *Revue de Metaphysique et de Morale*, 67:4 (October-December, 1962), pp. 410–30.

de Waelhens, Alphonse, *Une Philosophie de l'ambiguité: L'Existentialism de Maurice Merleau-Ponty*, Publications Universitaire de Louvain, 1951, Louvain.

———, '*Situation de Merleau-Ponty*,' *Les Temps Moderne*, 17:184–85 (October, 1961), pp. 377–98.

Wahl, Jean, 'Cette Pensee,' *Les Temps Moderne*, 17:184–85 (October, 1961), pp. 399–436.

Wertheimer, Max, *Productive Thinking*, Harper and Row, 1959, New York.

Index

Adler, Alfred, 4

Aesthetics: Heidegger's view of A. based upon a wrong conception of the thing, 43

Ambiguity: indicative of the human order of behavior, 28–29, 35

Amovable structure of behavior, 20–22

Analytic reflection, 125–126

Aristotle, 4–5, 142

Ballard, Edward G., 113

Being: (See also Flesh and Chiasm) related to thought for Heidegger, 125–126; evidenced by *écart*, 131–132; compared to Merleau-Ponty's notion of the unreflected, 135

Bergson, Henri, 60

Berio, Luciano, 117–118

Body: (See Body-image and Body-subject) objective body, 63–64; body as representation, 64

Body-image (*schéma corporel*): organized by directedness of body-subject, 85–86; accounts for gestural significance of verbal expression, 104;

Body-subject: suitability of term, 63; distinguished from the objective body and the body as representation, 63–64; teleology of, 66–67, 87; its pact with the natural world as a "primal acquisition," 76; its identity as a "pre-personal one," 78–80; directionality of, 80ff; parts defined by functionality of, 81–82; synergy of, 87; related to intersensoriality of

Body-subject (*Cont.*)
perceptual object, 86–87; as *je peux*, 94n, 105; relation to linguistic field as described by the *Fundierung* relation, 105ff.

Browning, Robert, 129

Cezanne, Paul, 64–66, 119

Chiasm: 10, relation to anatomical connotation, 134; c. between toucher and touched, 134–135; c. between seer and seen, 135–136; c. between touch and vision, 136–137; c. between moved and moving, 137–138; c. between speaking and listening, 138; c. between language and natural world, 138–141; distinguished from *Fundierung*, relation as conceived in Ph.P, 131; cannot be conceived in accordance with "representational thinking," 149ff.; in history, 154–155;

Darwin, on relation between gestural and linguistic expression, 103

Dehiscence: as a kind of *écart*, 140; descriptive of relation of levels of fields of difference, 153;

Descartes, R., 59, 124

Dimension, (See Levels), as descriptive of a relationship between fields, 123;

Dreyfus, H. L., 47, 161n

Écart: (See Chiasm)

Eidetic Reduction, 6–7, 127

El Greco, 13, 28

Empiricism: (See Epistemology)

Epistemology: empiricism and rationalism as epistemological types, 53; see Charts II and III, 54–56; ontological errors maintained by the empiricist and the rationalist, 52–53

Existentialism: *être au monde* (Merleau-Ponty) distinguished from being-in-the-world (Heidegger), 77; authenticity and "good faith" in Heidegger and Sartre, 90–93; "lighting" used as an ontological metaphor by existential writers, 94n; existence replaced by an "indirect ontology" in later work, 131;

Ferenczi, Sandor, 4

Fink, Eugene, 5–6, 11n, 38n

Flesh (*chair*): difficulty in translating *chair*, 141–142; as an ontological "element," 142; as expression of relation between a level and field of differences, 142–144; implies an "invisible" or "imperceived," 148–149; defined, 148–149; of things, 145–146; of expression, 146–148; cannot be conceived in accordance with "representational thinking," 149ff.; of history, 154–155;

Foucault, Michel, 4, 60–61; the *episteme* and Merleau-Ponty's later philosophy of history, 154;

Freud: explanation of psychopathological loss of speech, 90; on the overdetermination of the unconscious, 157–158; drive theory reinterpreted in terms of levels and fields of differences, 158–160;

Fundierung relation: 9; as defined in *The Logical Investigations*, 95–96; provides a revisionary concept of the "whole," 97–98; changed by Merleau-Ponty to express a relation between fields, 98–99; between eternity and time, 120; between reflected and unreflected, 123, distinguished from chiasm, 131

Gestalt: Merleau-Ponty's revision of the concept, 7–8, 14–16, 35–37; language described by concept of, 107, 110

Gestaltists: (Weisäcker, Goldstein, Koehler, and Koffka) 7, 33–35

Granel, G., 8

Hamlyn, D. W., 79

Haverkamp-Begemann, E., on *The Nightwatch*, 130

Hegel, G. W. F., 4–5

Heidegger, Martin: 2–3; errors in the ontology of the thing compared to *le préjugé du monde*, 61–71; thrownness (*Geworfenheit*) compared to Merleau-Ponty's "primal acquisition," 77; authenticity, 90, 92–93; authentic expression of H. and Merleau-Ponty, 111–112, 117; account of temporality distinguished from Merleau-Ponty's, 114–115; thinking compared to radical reflection, 125–126; on representational thinking, 149–151

Hemianopsia: pathological condition which does not admit the stimulus-response account, 17–18

Horizons: 24; elaboration of details in external h., 82–84; internal and external h. as polarization of the body-subject, 88–89; Husserl's definition of, 94n

Human order: definition of, 27–28

Husserl, Edmund: Merleau-Ponty's revision of H.'s concept of intentionality, 5–7, 33–37; phenomenological reduction, 6–7; eidetic reduction, 6–7, 127; the *Erfuellung* relation as alien to Merleau-Ponty's thought, 35; definition of external and internal horizons, 94n; H.'s notion of the body as a *le peux*, 94n; *Fundierung* relation revised by Merleau-Ponty, 95ff.; "pieces" and "moments" as described in the *Logical Investigations*, 96–98; definition of "whole,"

Husserl, Edmund (*Cont.*)
  97–98; Merleau-Ponty's rejection of H. on transcendental subjectivity, 99; account of temporality distinguished from Merleau-Ponty's, 118; H.'s failure to accept the unreflected as a background for the reflected, 127; on the reversibility of the body, 134;
Hyper-dialectic: 155–156

Intentionality: neither act nor operative agrees with Merleau-Ponty's sense of 9–10; act and operative intentionality are unsuitable to Merleau—Ponty's concept of the human order, 35
Introspection, 126

Kant, Immanuel, 59
Kaufmann, Walter, 2
Koehler, Wolfgang, 21–22
Koestler, Arthur, 37n
Koffka, Kurt, 25–26
Kohut, Heinz, 139, 161n

Lacan, Jacques, 139
Language: involvement with communal existence, 90; as gestural correlate of body, 102–105; allows neither sublimation nor reduction to body subject, 106; as a Gestalt, 107–108; authentic versus acquired expression, 110, 111–112, 117; Heidegger's view of authentic expression compared to Merleau—Ponty's, 111–112; *Fundierung* relation accounts for relation of language to the body-subject, 118; relation of authentic expression to temporality, 117–118; signified versus signifying aspects of l. 118–119; relation of acquired expression to temporality, 120; the "reversibility" of speaking and listening, 138;

Levels: (See also Dimensions) overall role of l. in perceptual constancies, 67; as optimum distance in size constancy, p. 68; as an atmospheric color in color constancy, 67–71; of verticality in shape constancy, 73–75; reconceived in later writings as an index of differences, 141–143ff.

Maclean, Paul D., 38n
Madison, Gary, 1–3, 115
Mallin, Samuel, 94n, 106, 126n
Marcel, Gabriel, 60
Meaning: irreducibility of m. as physiognomy in the pre-objective world, 47, 50–51, See Chart I, p. 50; m. of use-objects as polarized bodily skills, 79–80; sense of bodily parts determined by directedness of body-subject, 81–82; perception of distance as a polarization of the body-subject, 82–84; as difference (Saussure's diacritical theory), 106ff, 140;
Mind-body relation: accounted for through orders of behavior, 30–33; accounted for through the relation of levels to fields of difference, 155ff.
Mozart, W. A., 146–147
Mysticism: distinguished from Merleau-Ponty's "indirect ontology," 132

Nietzsche, Fredrich, 60, 61–62; on degrees of reality, 146;
The Nightwatch, the hand of the Captain as an example of Merleau-Ponty's theory of chiasm, 129–131
Novalis, 111

Paget, Richard, pantomimic theory of language, 103–4
Pears, David, 2
Perception: indeterminacy in, 48–49; sense-data theory, 57–58; size constancy, 67–68; (*maximum prise*), 68,

Perception: (*maximum prise*) (*Cont.*)
69, 88; color constancy, 68–72;
shape constancy, 72–76; primacy of
the perception of a thing over its
appearances, 76; weight constancy,
84–85; reversibility of toucher and
touched, 134–135, seer and seen,
135–136, touch and vision, 136–137,
moved and moving, 138 (See Chiasm);
Personal Intellectual Narrative: as a
background for understanding the
development of a philosopher's
thought, 2–9; Merleau-Ponty's referred to, 94n, 98–99
Phenomenological Reduction, 6–7
Plato: concept of color in the definition
of "figure" in the *Meno*, 70; gestural theory of language in the *Cratylus*, 102, 127n
le préjugé du monde, 10, 49–52, 54
Proust, Marcel, 29–30, 115–116, 147–148, 158, 161n.

Rabinow, Paul, 161n
Radical Reflection: criticism of r. r.
which implies a disinvolved subject,
112–114; based on a temporal relation, 114–116, 120–121; as a "perpetual beginning" initiated by authentic expression, 123; its relation
to the unreflected, 123–125;
Rationalism: (See Epistemology)
Rembrandt, shadows in *The Nightwatch*
as illustrative of Merleau-Ponty's
theory of the chiasm, 129–131;
Reversibility: (See Chiasm)
Rilke, Ranier-Maria, 128n
Rorty, Richard, 4

Sartre, Jean-Paul, 10, 77; on "bad
faith," 60, 90, 92; the elimination of
the Ego in *The Transcendence of the
Ego*, 97–98
Saussure, F: diacritical theory of language, 107–108, 140; influence of
Merleau-Ponty marked first in 1947,
107;

Scheler, Max, 23, 37n
Silverman, Hugh, 107
Stimulus-response theory: as a simple
causal account of behavior, 16–18
Subject-object relation: Heidegger's position distinguished from Merleau-Ponty's, 52
Symbolic structure of behavior, 32–35
Syncretic structure of behavior, 26–29
Synergy, 87

Temporality: the "original past" distinguished from Heidegger and Husserl's account of t., 114–115; Proust
on, 115–116; relation of authentic
expression of t., 117–118; relation of
acquired expression of t., 120; eternity and t., 120; role of t. in radical
reflection, 120–123; Rilke's "leave
taking" and Merleau—Ponty on t.,
128n
Thing: as substance and attribute, 43–46;
as collection of sensations, 46–47;
as matter and form, 47–49; intersensoriality of t. as reflective of the
synergy of the body-subject, 86–87
Thinking: related to Being for Heidegger, 125–126; Heidegger's view of
representational thinking as thinking
traditional conceived, 149–151;
Merleau-Ponty's later ontology requires that one thinks according to
differences and not according to
posited entities, 151–154;
Transitional synthesis, 76

Unconscious, as overdetermined, 157–158;

Valéry, Paul, 41–42

de Walhens, Alphonse, 113–114
World, as "unicity," 141;

170